COVID-19

200-400 DAYS

FACTS AND

FUN

Roberta Cava

Published by Cava Consulting

cavaconsulting@ozemail.com.au

www.dealingwithdifficultpeople.info

Cava, Roberta

Covid-19

200-400 Days

Facts and Fun

National Library of Australia
Cataloguing-in-publication data:

ISBN: 9780645076202

BOOKS BY ROBERTA CAVA

All can be purchased from Amazon Books

Non-Fiction

Dealing with Difficult People
(International best-seller since 1990 with 24 publishers – in 18 languages in over 100 countries)
Kein Problem mit Schwierigen Menschen (German)
Tratando con Gente Difícil (Spanish)
Traiter avec des personnes difficiles (French)
Comunicareaea cu oameni dificili (Romanian)

Dealing with Difficult Situations – at Work and at Home
Tratando con Situationes Dificiles (Spanish)

Dealing with Difficult Spouses and Children
Tratando con Cónyuges y Niños Difíciles

Dealing with Difficult Relatives and In-Laws
Tratando con parientes difíciles y en leyes

Dealing with School Bullying
Tratando con la Intimidación en la Escouela (Spanish)

Dealing with Workplace Bullying
Tratando con Intimidación en el lugar de trabajo

Keeping Our Children Safe
Mantenera Nuestros Hijos Seguros (Spanish)

Dealing with Domestic Violence and Child Abuse
Retirement Village Bullies
Just say no
What am I going to do with the rest of my life?
Interpersonal Communication at Work
Change? Not me!
Creative Problem-Solving & Decision-Making
Customer Service that Works
Teambuilding
How Women can advance in business
Before Tying the Knot – Questions couples must ask each other before they marry!

Survival Skills for Supervisors and Managers
Human Resources at its Best!
Human Resources Policies and Procedures - Australia
Employee Handbook
Easy Come – Hard to go – The Art of Hiring, Disciplining and Firing Employees
Time and Stress – Today's silent killers
Take Command of your Future – Make things Happen!
The Presenter
Belly Laughs for All! – Volumes 1 to 8
Australian Trivia
Trivia and More
Wisdom of the World! The happy, sad & wise things in life!
Covid-19 200 Days – Facts and Fun
Covid-19 200-400 Days – Facts and Fun

Fiction

I can do it! The sky's the limit!
Twists and Turns
Treacherous Livelihoods
Life Gets Complicated
Life Goes On
Life Gets Better
That Something Special
Something Missing

COVID-19
200-400 DAYS
FACTS AND FUN

Table of Contents

INTRODUCTION

This book is a sequel to my *COVID-19 200 Days – Facts and Fun* book released in August 2020.

The entire world is still in the throes of fighting the pandemic, but most people are anxiously awaiting the roll-out of the many COVID-19 vaccines. International travel is at a minimum and will likely continue until the end of 2021 with those who travel likely needing a 'vaccine passport' to prove that they have had one of the vaccines. Unfortunately, there are still many people who are anti-vaxxers who will likely be kept homebound rather than be allowed to travel.

There were giant surges of cases in the US due to poor leadership by President Donald Trump who, as the leader of the Republican Party (formerly known as GOP – Grand Old Party) spent much of the year downplaying the threat of the virus that has killed 517,204 Americans by the end of 400 days. One of his claims for re-election was that the coronavirus dangers had been blown out of proportion.

Donald Trump ran America as if it was a business and to hell with his employees (constituents).

Joe Biden the present reigning President and leader of the Democratic Party, has been diligent in wearing a mask and encouraged all others to do the same along with proper handwashing and practicing social distancing. He made Trump's frequent downplaying of the pandemic and mixed messaging on mask-wearing a central campaign theme for the November 3rd election in 2020.

CHAPTER 1

THE FACTS

The first 200 days ended on August 12, 2020, but new information surfaced a month earlier and wasn't reported. This edition of COVID-19 goes from August 13, 2020 until March 1, 2021.

I mentioned the following information in my first book, but think it is wise to include it in this book as well for people who may not have read the first book. It is the facts relating to COVID-19:

July 16 - **London** – It has been determined that headaches are the most common symptom of coronavirus, with 62% of patients who show any COVID-19 symptoms. Research by the Imperial College of London found that loss of taste or smell were each more common than a persistent cough. 50% of those interviewed said that having a blocked nose was the second most common symptom in the week before testing positive. Diarrhoea affected exactly one third of those who experienced any symptoms, while loss of smell and taste affected 30% and 28% respectively. Fever affected only 20% who reported symptoms and a new persistent cough 23%.

The data come from more than 120,000 volunteers aged over five across Britain in May. Only three in ten people testing positive for the virus showed any symptoms at all.

These findings show how COVID-19 was able to sweep through the British population before lockdown was ordered towards the end of March.

The research found young adults aged 18 - 24 were more likely to test positive than other age groups.

COVID info from John Hopkins Hospital

This virus is not a living organism. It is a protein molecule (RNA or DNA) covered by a protective layer of lipid (fat), which, when absorbed by the cells of the ocular (eyes), nasal (nose) or buccal mucosa (mouth), changes their genetic code (mutates) and converts into aggressor and multiplier cells.

Since the virus is not a living organism, but is a protein molecule, it has to decay on its own. The disintegration time depends on the temperature, humidity, and type of material where it lies. The virus

3

is very fragile; the only thing that protects it is a thin outer layer of fat and that is the reason why soap or detergent is the best weapon. The foam cuts the fat (that is why you have to scrub for 20 seconds or more, to create lots of foam). By dissolving the fat layer, the protein molecule disperses and breaks down.

You have to wash your hands before and after touching any commonly used surfaces such as: mucosa (mouth area), food, packages, locks, knobs, switches, remotes, cell phones, watches, gasoline pumps, computers, desks, etc. You have to moisturize your hands due to frequent washing. Dry hands have cracks, and the molecules can hide in the micro cracks. The thicker the moisturizer, the better. Also keep your nails short so that the virus does not hide there.

Heat melts fat. This is why use water above 77 degrees for hand washing, laundry and cleaning surfaces. In addition, hot water makes more foam, making it more effective. Alcohol or any mixture with alcohol over 65% dissolves all fat, especially the external lipid layer of the virus.

Any solution with one-part bleach and 5 parts water directly dissolves the protein, breaking it down from the inside. Oxygenated water increases the effectiveness of soap, alcohol and chlorine, because peroxide dissolves the virus protein. However, because you have to use it in its pure form, it can damage your skin. Vinegar is not useful because it does not break down the protective layer of fat. As spirits and vodka are only 40% alcohol, and you need a minimum of 65%. Even 110 proof won't work. Listerine is okay because it is 65% alcohol.

No bactericide or antibiotic will work because the virus is not a living organism like bacteria; antibodies cannot kill what is not alive. The virus molecules remain very stable at colder temperatures, including air conditioning in houses and cars. They also need moisture and darkness to stay stable. Therefore, dehumidified, dry, warm and bright environments will degrade the virus faster. UV light on any object that may contain the virus breaks down the protein. Be careful, it also breaks down collagen (which is protein) in the skin.

The virus cannot go through healthy skin.

A higher concentration of the virus is found in more confined spaces. The more open or naturally ventilated, the less the concentration.

Warning: *I'd like to add a word of caution here – if you are using a hand sanitizer – be aware that it has a high alcohol content and is inflammable. If you use a sanitizer and then light a candle or cigarette – your hands could catch fire.*

Differences between COVID-19 and other viruses

SARS-CoV-2 is the virus that causes COVID-19. Coronavirus can be difficult to detect because it mimics the symptoms of other viruses including the flu. However, there is a certain order in which COVID-19 symptoms occur. A paper by researchers from the University of South California (USC), is based on the symptoms of more than 55,000 confirmed cases of COVID-19.

The researchers found the initial symptoms often appear in the following specific order:

1. Fever
2. Cough
3. Nausea and/or vomiting
4. Diarrhoea

This order differs only slightly from other respiratory illnesses, but there's a critical difference that might help with the detection of COVID-19. If you have contracted influenza (the flu), the first symptom you will observe is a cough - not a fever.

"This order is especially important to know when we have overlapping cycles of illnesses like the flu that coincide with infections of COVID-19," said researcher Peter Kuhn, professor of medicine and biomedical engineering at USC.

There is also a subtle difference in the timing of COVID-19 symptoms when compared to Middle East Respiratory Syndrome (MERS) and Severe Acute Respiratory Syndrome (SARS).

The upper gastrointestinal (GI) tract seems to be affected before the lower GI tract in COVID-19 cases which is the opposite to MERS and SARS.

This is why nausea and vomiting often presents before diarrhoea among some COVID-19 patients.

Here is what happened world-wide after August 7, 2020:

August 7 - **New Zealand** - Scientists at the **University of Otago** released a surprising new study today which revealed where New Zealand's early cases of coronavirus came from. The researchers analysed the genomic sequencing of 649 people infected with COVID-19 between February 26 and May 22 - representing 56 percent of all confirmed cases during that time. The sequences could quickly tell the team where each specific case of COVID-19 came from and pick it apart from other cases in the community.

The study, led by Dr Jemma Geoghegan, revealed most cases in New Zealand originated from North America rather than Asia where the virus first emerged. They said this is "likely reflecting the high prevalence of the virus in North America during the sampling period."

- **India** has the third highest COVID-19 caseload in the world. India has recorded 933 COVID-19 fatalities in the past 24 hours as fresh infections surged by another 61,537 cases to reach nearly 2.1 million. The Health Ministry says the total deaths reached 42,518, including more than 20,000 in the past 30 days. An average of around 50,000 new cases are reported each day since mid-June.

August 8 - **Dublin Ireland** reported 174 new cases of COVID-19, by far the highest number of infections since May and up from 98 on yesterday and an average of 58 cases per day for the past week.

Chief Medical Officer Ronan Glynn said 118 of the new cases were linked to the three counties - Kildare, Laois and Offaly - where some restrictions on movement were reintroduced yesterday following a surge in cases there.

August 10 - **Paris** - Wearing a face mask will be compulsory in busy parts of Paris from today amid a rise in coronavirus infections in and around the French capital. Police said the order would apply to people aged 11 and over in 'certain very crowded zones.' The virus had been circulating more widely in the region since mid-July, they said. Face masks are already compulsory in enclosed public spaces. Experts have warned that France could lose control of Covid-19 'at any time.'

Several cities, such as Nice and Lille, have introduced their own additional orders making mask-wearing mandatory in certain outdoor areas. They added that 400 people were testing positive for coronavirus every day in the region, with those aged between 20 and 30 particularly affected.

August 14 - **New Zealand** – 13 new cases in a cluster.

 - Now over 20 million cases **Globally.**

 - **China** - It was the first country to experience an outbreak of COVID-19, and the country where it was first detected, giving Chinese researchers a head start on developing a vaccine to fight the disease which has now killed more than 773,649 people around the world.

One vaccine under development by the pharmaceutical firm CanSino and the People's Liberation Army has already been cleared for use by the nation's military personnel. But given the Chinese Communist Party-led nation's prickly foreign relations with many Western nations, including Australia, questions have been raised over what would happen if China were to become the first country to develop an effective vaccine. Chinese President Xi Jinping has said his country's vaccines would be a 'global public good' and would be made available to all nations.

However, questions have also been raised about the quality of Chinese-produced vaccines, in the face of multiple scandals in the country's vaccine manufacturing industry in the past decade.

August 14 - As lockdown measures lifted in the **UK,** the sun came out and many Brits seized their opportunity for a much-needed summer escape.

While an overseas holiday might seem like a distant dream for many Australians, British tourists have been enjoying idyllic destinations in **Spain** and **France**. However, it's all come to an abrupt end when more cases erupted in **Spain** last month and forced all returnees to go into quarantine for 14 days.

 - **France, Malta** and the **Netherlands** joined the list. Many returnees will now have to add 14 days to their vacation time and remain in quarantine. I'm sure their bosses are not happy about this.

Anyone contemplating a trip must ask themselves: Is it worth going overseas if it results in two weeks in isolation?

Some countries are exploring other options to get around quarantine. One of these options is doing rapid testing which can reduce their quarantine period to as little as one day. Most test results are given withing 24-48 hours and if the test is negative, they can leave quarantine.

Germans who holiday overseas are offered a free test at the airport the moment they return home. The German government pays for those tests.

Travellers from high-risk locations will still be tested and ordered to go into quarantine.

France, Greece and **Iceland** have their own test-on-arrival programs.

In the **UK**, approval is still pending for a trial that could give passengers at London's Heathrow airport their results in just seven hours, at a cost of roughly 157GBP.

- **New Zealand** reported seven new cases as a lockdown in the country's biggest city, Auckland, was extended on August 13 in response to the country's first coronavirus outbreak in months.

Six of the seven new cases have been linked to the cluster responsible for all the previous community cases, while one case is being investigated.

The new cases bring New Zealand's total infections since the start of the year to 1,258, while the number of currently active cases stands at 56. Twenty -two people have died so far.

The lockdown in Auckland was extended for nearly two weeks following the discovery on August 11 of the country's first COVID-19 infections in 102 days, in a family in Auckland.

The New Zealand's Prime Minister **Jacinda Ardern** is now being accused by her opposition [the National Party] of failing to secure quarantine facilities and for withholding information.

Here is more information relating to this outbreak: "We can report that the outbreak in Auckland is being investigated by both the Police and the Department of Corrections.

"We have been informed that the 20 something daughter of the South Auckland family concerned, visited her boyfriend (or associate) who was in quarantine having recently been deported from Australia for criminal behaviour. The boyfriend has COVID-19 and has passed this on to the daughter via their meeting which is believed to have taken place at an Auckland quarantine site.

The daughter, who is currently unemployed and well-known to police, was given a substantial amount of cash by this person. It is this cash that funded their travels around the North Island, particularly Rotorua with her young child. The pair stayed at the expensive Wai Ora Lake Resort and splurged cash on many other luxuries normally outside the means of the family.

Police are currently working with the Department of Corrections to try and map the daughter's movements. She is apparently well known to both government agencies and is not necessarily cooperating with investigators.

We can confirm that this information was provided to us by a member of one of those agencies direct. The media is aware of the story but has been asked not to report it in order to stem public anger."

August 18 - **South Africa**, which had one of the world's strictest lockdowns for five months, has begun relaxing restrictions in response to decreasing new cases and hospitalisations for COVID-19.

The country loosened its regulations today, permitting the sales of alcohol and cigarettes and allowing the opening of bars, restaurants, gyms, and places of worship, all limited to no more than 50 people. Virtually all businesses and factories have reopened with distancing regulations.

Schools will re-open gradually from August 24, starting with grades 12 and 7 and a phased opening of other grades. The country will keep its night-time curfew from 10:00 pm to 4:00 am.

With more than 589,000 confirmed cases, South Africa, has more than half of all reported cases in Africa, and more than 11,900 deaths from COVID-19.

South Africa's new confirmed cases have dropped from an average of 12,000 per day at the peak in July to less than 5,000 per day last week.

- **Seoul** - South Korean health officials are struggling to contain an outbreak of the coronavirus, as new cases levelled off but remained in triple digits on August 13.

The Korea Centers for Disease Control and Prevention (KCDC) reported 288 new cases as of midnight today, marking at least a week of triple digit daily increases.

Overall, South Korea has reported 16,346 cases with 307 deaths.

August 19 – **World Health Organization** (WHO) chief Tedros Adhanom Ghebreyesus says countries putting their own interests ahead of those of others in trying to ensure supplies of vaccines are making the pandemic worse.

"Nationalism exacerbated the pandemic and contributed to the total failure of the global supply chain," he said. He said he had sent a letter to all WHO members asking them to join the multilateral COVAX vaccine effort.

A Chinese pharmaceutical company has revealed that a potential vaccine it is developing is likely to cost less than $200 for two doses.

- **Brazil's** Vice-President, Hamilton Mourao, has defended his Government's response to the coronavirus pandemic, saying a lack of discipline from his compatriots made the Government's job more difficult. The South American nation is the world's second worst for coronavirus cases and deaths after the United States.

"Of course, we regret the deaths of more than 100,000 Brazilians, but the Federal Government and the state governments did everything we could," Mr. Mourao told the BBC.

"We were successful in adapting the curve of the pandemic to the capacity of our public hospitals. In the beginning everybody was afraid that we would have people dying in the halls of our hospitals, and this did not happen. "We had a lot of measures to mitigate the economic and social problems. I think we are doing a good job."

Mr. Mourao said Brazilians by nature were "not very disciplined," so it's impossible to come from the top down and say, 'You have to do this, you have to do that,'" he said.

Brazil's President Jair Bolsonaro has repeatedly played down the seriousness of COVID-19, describing it as "a little flu." [More head-burying.]

August 30 – **London** – Boris Johnson's approval rating has fallen to the lowest since last October. 53% of people said they had an unfavourable view of Mr. Johnson – with 38% in favour.

In the **UK**, as many as 60% of respondents of a YourGov survey said they definitely or probably would not get vaccinated.

In **France** – One in four people said they wouldn't get a coronavirus vaccine when it's found.

In the **US** – one-third of Americans don't want to be vaccinated against COVID-19.

September 1 - **South Africa** has registered more than half a million confirmed cases of Covid-19, health officials have said, as the government struggles to retain public trust amid allegations of widespread corruption, arbitrary decisions on restrictions and administrative incompetence.

Africa's most industrialised nation was widely praised for its early response to the pandemic, but criticism has since mounted as a strict lockdown was eased.

"The lockdown succeeded in delaying the spread of the virus by more than two months, preventing a sudden and uncontrolled increase in infections in late March," the South African president, Cyril Ramaphosa, said on August 29th in the latest in a series of televised speeches to the nation.

September 5 – **India** – 86,432 new cases. Total cases so far over 4 million. Total deaths - 69,561.

September 7 – As the southern hemisphere warms up, we could see a drop in the transmission of the virus even though Florida and Brazil saw an explosion of cases during their summer months. More sunlight, warmth and more humidity will help, and people should spent more time outdoors.

As the northern hemisphere cools off, we could see a rise in the transmission of the virus. Chia, USA and Italy were hit hard during their winter.

- One of the world's leading obstetric fistula surgeons, Dr. Andrew Browning (based in Sydney) has been given special government approval to make a mercy dash to Africa to aid a community of children dying from severe malnutrition as a result of COVID-19.

September 8 – **India** – 90,000 new cases. Total deaths now 72,816.

September 17 – **Hong Kong** – Doctor Li-Meng Yan, who published a study undermining the origin theory that coronavirus naturally occurred, told Fox News it did not come from nature.

"This is created in the lab," she told Fox News.

"China's military discovered and owned the very unique bat coronavirus which cannot affect people, but after the modification became the very harmful virus.

"I have evidence to show why they can do it, what they have done, how did they do it."

She said nobody speaks about the virus being manufactured in China because of 'big suppression' from the Chinese Communist Party.

"The scientific world also keeps silent, works together with Chinese Community Party," Dr Li-Meng said. "They don't want people to know this truth."

"That's why I get suspended, I get suppression, I am the target that the Chinese Community Party wants to be disappeared. I worked in the WHO reference lab which is the top coronavirus lab in the world at the University of Hong Kong. And the thing is I get deeply into such investigation in secret from the early beginning of this outbreak. I had my intelligence because I also get my own unit network in China."

In her research, the doctor said SARS-CoV-2, the virus which causes COVID-19, shows "biological characteristics that are inconsistent with a naturally occurring zoonotic virus" and could be created in a lab in "approximately six months."

"The natural origin theory, although widely accepted, lacks substantial support," the authors said.

"The alternative theory that the virus may have come from a research laboratory is, however, strictly censored on peer-reviewed scientific journals. The genomic, structural, medical, and literature evidence, which, when considered together, strongly contradicts the natural origin theory. The evidence shows that SARS-CoV-2 should be a laboratory product created by using bat coronaviruses ZC45 and/or ZXC21 as a template and/or backbone."

Dr. Li-Meng said she would release another report soon to "make you fully understand the case."

Her research was uploaded to the open-access repository website Zenodo.

https://www.foxnews.com/world/chinese-virologist-coronavirus-cover-up-flee-hong-kong-whistleblower

September 18 – **UK** Government scientists have warned of a 'developing situation' over people bringing coronavirus into the UK after travelling abroad and returning home without being tested.

People who travel overseas are required to quarantine for two weeks on their return unless they have visited a country on the official list of nations considered low risk for Covid-19.

However, the lack of testing at airports and other borders along with poor compliance with quarantine has resulted in infected travellers spreading the virus when they get home - even if they test positive and self-isolate later.

Experts on the government's scientific advisory committee, warned that while imported infections were a small proportion of UK cases - they still are a threat.

In a statement dated September 2nd but released in a bundle of Sage documents on September 18th, the group decided that testing at borders was unlikely to prevent returning travellers from starting fresh outbreaks. But the measures could provide valuable surveillance for inbound infection and help remind people of the need to quarantine.

Speaking to MPs on the parliamentary science and technology committee this week, Lord Bethell, the Minister for Innovation, said, "Work on testing arriving travellers was ongoing with the Department of Transport, airlines and airports, but that the quarantine advice from Prof. Chris Whitty, England's chief medical officer, was clear. 'We've already had very tough outcomes from people coming into the country bringing disease with them, and we have to rely on people complying with quarantine, and the evidence suggests that that is a very difficult thing to rely upon," Bethell said.

There have been calls from the travel industry and some Tory MPs to bring in airport testing and reduce quarantine times to allow more travel for holidays and business.

In the summer, science advisers realised that thousands of cases, mostly from **France** and **Spain**, had been imported into the UK in February and March, seeding outbreaks around the country.

"Although testing at borders is unlikely to have significant impact on importation rates, it would provide important epidemiological surveillance data and potentially reduce onwards transmission if it results in higher adherence to quarantine periods and activating onwards contact tracing," the statement adds.

In another document released today, the minutes of a Sage meeting on September 3rd, advisors cautioned that the proportion of people with antibodies against coronavirus, about 6% nationally, was unlikely to reduce the impact of a winter resurgence.

With the second wave building, the committee called for public-health messaging to explain that people are at risk of getting Covid-19 twice and must still isolate even if they have had the virus before.

Further minutes from a Sage meeting on August 27th called for caution over mass testing. The advisors said the approach was most likely to work in well-defined, high-risk settings, such as care homes and meat processing plants, where large outbreaks could be caught early. But mass testing, through pooled saliva samples, could backfire in areas with little virus around because false positive rates could reduce public confidence in testing.

September 18 – **UK** –"People in England who break the new rule that requiring them to self-isolate if they have been in contact with someone infected with COVID-19 will be fined," Prime Minister Boris Johnson said. Fines will start at 1,000 pounds for a first offence and rise to 10,000 pounds for repeat offenders or cases where employers threaten to sack staff who self-isolate rather than work.

The rules will apply from September 28 to anyone in England who tests positive for the virus or is notified by public health workers that they have been in contact with someone infectious.

September 19 – **India** has the fastest-growing outbreak in the world, with almost 100,000 new cases recorded daily and five million cases in total. It is about to overtake the US as the country worst-hit by the virus. 25 MPs have tested positive for COVID-19.

September 22 - **Wales** will have strict limits on travelling and socialising will start at 6:00 pm tonight. Affected areas are Newport, Bridgend, Merthyr Tydfil and Blaenau Gwent in South Wales. Lockdowns are already in place in Caerphilly and Rhondda Cynon Taf. Government officials pointed out that other local restrictions or even a national lockdown could be brought in.

– **Global deaths** from COVID-19 rose closer to 1 million.

- **UK** – Reports indicate that the UK is considering a second nation-wide lockdown.

- **US** – Now has 202,409 deaths. Johns Hopkins University data shows that new coronavirus cases have increased in about two-thirds of the states in the US.

September 23 - Prime Minister Boris Johnson addressed the **United Kingdom** today, announcing a new coronavirus package rolling out "tougher measures" to combat a surge in cases across the nation.

"While the vast majority have complied with the rules, there have been too many breaches, too many opportunities for our invisible enemy to slip through undetected," Mr. Johnson said.

"The virus has started to spread again in an exponential way: infections are up, hospital bills are climbing.

The prime minister said the new restrictions would include, "Early closing for pubs, bars, table service only, closing businesses that are not COVID secure, expanding the use of face coverings and new fines for those that fail to comply."

September 27 – Discussions have been made about allowing flights between **Australia** and **New Zealand.** The plan would permit New Zealand residents to fly to NSW with no quarantine period required and NSW residents would be allowed to travel to NZ by Christmas.

Federal Tourism Minister Simon Birmingham said, "We are still hopeful that travel could be speeded up with NZ this year." Transport and Tourism Forum chief executive Margy Osmond said flights between Sydney and Auckland could resume by November.

October 8 – **Wuhan** - Just six months ago, Wuhan was emerging from the world's first - and one of its strictest lockdowns.

Wuhan has welcomed more than 18 million tourists. About 640 million travellers injected $96 billion into the economy. Experts say citizens have "no choice but to obey" Beijing's coronavirus measures.

But during China's Golden Week earlier this month, the streets of Wuhan, once ground zero for COVID-19, were bustling with tourists.

The city welcomed more than 18 million tourists during Golden Week from October 1 to 8, according to official data from the Wuhan Tourism Bureau.

Golden Week is a week-long holiday to celebrate the country's National Day, and it typically generates a surge in tourism - almost all of it domestic in 2020 due to international border closures.

Some 637 million Chinese tourists travelled for Golden Week this year, injecting 466.6 billion Chinese yuan into the economy, according to the Chinese Ministry of Culture and Tourism.

October 18 – **Paris** – European leaders have ordered new lockdowns trying to prevent another wave of COVID-19 cases. People have been refusing to comply. French cities announced that an anti-virus curfew will take effect. Marseille's mayor Michele Rubinola (a doctor) said the curfew was costing residents 'their daily pleasures and their freedom.'

Worldwide, more than 400,000 new cases were reported yesterday.

In **Europe,** the average number of daily infections has risen 44% in a single week to over 121,000.

Belgian Deputy Prime Minister Georges Gilkinet announced that bars and restaurants would close for four weeks starting on Monday, October 19.

UK Prime Minister Boris Johnson attacked the mayor of Greater Manchester, Andy Burnham, saying that more people would die for each day they refused to go into a full lockdown.

In **Berlin,** irate restaurant owners successfully challenged court order to close bars and restaurants after 11:00 pm. Judges agreed that it was not apparent that such a measure could fight the virus.

A **World Health Organisation** backed study found that the antiviral drug Remdesivir, considered one of the most promising COVID-19 treatments, turns out to do little to prevent deaths from the disease.

Remdesivir, which was part of the experimental cocktail given the US President Donald Trump when he caught the virus last month, was one of several reviewed in a large study of more than 11,000 people across 30 countries.

"The drug, 'appeared to have little or no effect on hospitalized cases, as indicated by overall mortality, initiation of ventilation and duration of hospital stay," said the study posted online. This study appears to contradict at least two major US studies.

October 19 - The **Irish government** agreed during a Cabinet meeting today to move the country to level five restrictions in a bid to combat the rise in cases of COVID-19.

Irish premier Michael Martin said the Government was introducing Level 5 restrictions for the entire country because 'the evidence of a potentially grave situation arising in the weeks ahead was now too strong.' The new restrictions will come into force from midnight on Wednesday October 21st and are set to last until December 1.

He said schools and creches would remain open because, "We cannot and will not allow our children and young people's futures to be another victim of this disease. They need their education."

Under the new measures no social or family gatherings are allowed in homes or gardens but visits on compassionate grounds and for caring purposes can continue.

October 21 - On January 25, something strange started happening in China's crematoriums – proving **Beijing** wasn't telling the truth about its virus cases.

Discrepancies in Beijing's COVID-19 reporting have been raising suspicions world-wide since January. A new study of Chinese medical, media and bureaucratic reports points to a massive cover-up of the outbreak's severity.

A new study accuses Beijing as hiding the number of infections and deaths from the pandemic which had a severe impact on how the world responded to the outbreak.

The study, which is yet to undergo the scientific quality-control process of peer review, was published on the medRxiv early release service.

The first official recognition of the virus outbreak was from Wuhan city in early January. But news of the strange new pneumonia-like disease began to appear on Chinese medical forums in late December. Beijing immediately cracked down on the discussion and silenced the doctors involved.

By late January, Wuhan's hospitals were reported to be under severe strain. They offered 90,000 beds and another 100,000 beds were activated in hotels and schools. Yet Beijing's figures reported only 33,000 COVID-19 cases.

By March 23, 42,600 doctors and healthcare workers had been rushed to Wuhan from other provinces to support the 90,000 already there. But Beijing reported only 50,000 cases.

Before Beijing's crackdown, China's bureaucracy had been conducting business as usual – analysing, assessing and reporting on everything about its citizenry. The researchers from Washington University and Ohio State University say they tracked down this early government data and combined it with reports in state-controlled and social media.

Among this information were the activities of eight crematories in Wuhan. By January 25 these were inexplicably operating around the clock. Based on such sources, the researchers argue the total number of infections and fatalities before February was at least ten times that of the official figure announced by Beijing.

 - **Czech Republic** – had a spike in new cases – 8,713 in 1 day with 67 deaths.

- **Global** cases now 40,652,097 up 5,640,775 since October 1st. Deaths 1,122,036 up 87,171 since October 1st.

October 27 - There were more than 500,000 new cases of COVID-19 recorded worldwide today - a record, according to Agence France-Press. The total was 516,898 cases and 7,723 fatalities, according to an AFP tally.

- **European** countries set a series of records today, and World Health Organization's head of emergencies, Dr. Michael Ryan, warned this week that Europe has again become the epicentre. New cases rose – in Poland 18,820, the Czech Republic 15,663 Germany with 14,964, Switzerland with 8,616, Slovenia with 2,605, Russia with a record 346 deaths and 16,202 new cases, and Ukraine with 165 deaths and 7,474 new cases.

- **Germany** and **France** were set to announce new lock-downs as both countries grapple with surges in new cases. French President Emmanuel Macron slated to address the nation later today and to announce a one-month lockdown.

October 28 - The **UK** has recorded 367 more COVID-19 deaths in the latest 24-hour period, official figures show. It is the highest daily figure since May 27, when 422 fatalities were reported. Yesterday, it was announced 102 people had died within 28 days of a positive COVID-19 test. There were 45,365 coronavirus deaths, according to government data.

A further 22,885 laboratory-confirmed COVID-19 cases have been announced in the latest 24-hour period, taking the total to 917,575. October 26th number of infections was 20,890.

There were 670 fatalities registered in England and Wales which mentioned 'novel coronavirus' in the week ending 16 October. This is a rise of 53% from the previous week, when 438 deaths involving COVID-19 were registered. It is the sixth successive rise and the highest number of registered deaths involving coronavirus since the week ending 19 June.

Dr. Yvonne Doyle, medical director of Public Health England, warned the rising number of deaths was likely to continue for some time. "Each day we see more people testing positive and hospital admissions increasing."

October 31 – **US** - New cases today topped 89,223.

– A second lockdown looms as cases spike in **UK**. A health expert explained that Boris Johnson has 'little choice' but to impose more restrictions.

It appears that two of the people in line for the British throne: Prince Charles and Prince William both had Covid-19 in April. If they had died it would have left the next in line for the British throne to be young Prince George who was only seven at that time.

Shortly before that, on 27 March, the British Prime Minister, Boris Johnson was very ill with Covid as well, so Britain had a close call regarding the leadership of the country.

November 2 - The **UK** recorded 397 deaths from coronavirus today - the biggest daily toll since May. New cases of the virus rose, with 20,018 recorded as of 9:00 am on November 3rd, compared to 18,950 for the previous 24 hours. Their new lockdown will begin on November 5th and last until December 2.

November 15 – **UK** - Boris Johnson must self-isolate after being in touch with someone who has tested positive for Covid-19. On November 12th, the Prime Minister held a 35-minute meeting with a group of MPs including Lee Anderson who later tested positive for the virus.

Mr. Johnson has no symptoms of Covid-19 and will continue to work from Downing Street, his official spokesperson said. Under Government guidelines, those who come into contact with people who test positive must isolate for 14 days.

November 18 – **France** has topped 2 million cases.

- **Russia -** President Vladimir Putin has won a resounding victory in his bid to stay in power until the middle of the next decade, as Russians voted overwhelmingly to endorse the country's political status quo, according to preliminary results.

Russia went to the polls today to cast ballots in a nationwide referendum on constitutional amendments. The vote paves the way for Putin, who has ruled for two decades, to remain president until 2036.

November 22 – The University of Oxford has advised that individuals infected with coronavirus are not likely to catch the illness again for at least six months.

November 23 - Prime Minister Boris Johnson announced details of lockdown plans for December in the House of Commons, setting out the rules for the festive period. The winter strategy includes a newly strengthened three tier system of local restrictions, with Leeds expected to be placed back into Tier 3.

Under the original tier system, England was divided into Tier 1 (medium alert), Tier 2 (high alert) and Tier 3 (very high alert). Unlike the previous arrangements, tiers will be a uniform set of rules meaning local authorites won't be able to negotiate restrictions for their region.

Areas in Tier 1 were subject to the same national measures that were in force nationally, including a 10:00 pm curfew for pubs and restaurants, and a ban on gatherings of more than six people.

Tier 2 areas saw a ban on household mixing indoors, but the rule of six continued to apply outdoors. In Tier 2, pubs will only be able to serve alcohol as part of a 'substantial meal,' and customers must stay within their household groups. This rule previously only applied in Tier 3.

Areas in Tier 3 were subject to the strictest rules, with household mixing banned indoors and in private gardens, and pubs and restaurants closed, unless they could operate as a restaurant.

Ministers will announce which areas will be placed into Tier 1, Tier 2 and Tier 3 on Thursday 26 November.

November 24 - **Singapore** now requires incoming travellers over the age of 12 to wear electronic monitoring devices if they're not staying in a dedicated quarantine facility, while **Hong Kong** has a similar policy.

Papua New Guinea recently made ankle bracelets mandatory for international workers arriving in the country on designated charter flights, which must be worn while they're in two weeks quarantine.

Jet setting **Australians** will have to comply with strict new rules when international flights finally return to the skies post-coronavirus, Qantas boss Alan Joyce has warned. From ankle bracelets to DNA tests, sewage testing on planes and mandatory vaccinations. Overseas travel will never be the same again.

Mr. Joyce revealed his airline will overhaul its terms and conditions for travel where a coronavirus vaccination will be a compulsory requirement for passengers heading abroad, which could be as early as next year.

- **Qatar's** public prosecutor has filed criminal charges against an unspecified number of police officers working at Qatar's Hamad airport after a number of Australian women said they were invasively searched there last month.

Prosecutors in Qatar say the airport police officers who ordered forced internal medical examinations of female passengers after an abandoned newborn was discovered in a rubbish bin, face possible three-year prison sentences.

Prosecutors did not say how many police officers at Hamad International Airport faced charges over the October 2 incident that sparked widespread anger in Australia, a key destination for the state-owned Qatar Airways. The physical examinations of passengers bound for Sydney and nine other unnamed destinations triggered outrage in Australia. The government denounced the searches as inappropriate and beyond circumstances in which the women could give free and informed consent.

"Extensive investigations revealed that some employees of the Airport Security Department acted unilaterally by summoning female medical staff to conduct external examination to some female passengers, thinking that what they had done was within the law," a statement from prosecutors said.

Qatar has this morning confirmed they have identified the newborn's parents and are attempting to extradite the mother. The abandoned newborn's mother, whom the statement described as a 'convict,' faces up to 15 years in prison if apprehended. The woman apparently flew out of the country before the baby was discovered.

November 29 – **Sweden** – is in the midst of a second wave with triple the mortality rate of its Scandinavian neighbours.

December 2 - People can catch COVID-19 twice. That's the emerging consensus among health experts who are learning more about the possibility that those who've recovered from the coronavirus can get it again. So far, the phenomenon doesn't appear to be widespread - with a few hundred reinfection cases reported worldwide - yet those numbers are likely to expand as the pandemic continues.

- **UK** - Boris Johnson suffered the largest backbench rebellion of his premiership yesterday after more than 50 Tory Members of Parliament voted against the new three-tier system of coronavirus regulations.

The measures were passed by 291 votes to 78, paving the way for 99 per cent of England to be placed under the toughest Tier 2 and 3 restrictions when England's national lockdown ends at midnight.

- A global alliance of more than 200 MPs from 19 countries has launched a campaign urging people around the world to buy Australian wine in response to China's 'bullying.'

The Inter-Parliamentary Alliance on China launched the crusade after Beijing slapped Australian wine with tariffs of up to 212 per cent – a roadblock Trade Minister Simon Birmingham said would render the country's market 'unviable.'

December 11 - Acclaimed **South Korean** film director Kim Ki-duk, who won global recognition for his violent works and faced allegations of abusing his actresses, died from coronavirus in Latvia on Friday, the country's top film official said.

His movies - many featuring gruesome violence against both males and females, and rapes of women - divided audiences, with some accusing him of misogyny and others hailing his cinematography and unflinching portrayal of a social underclass rarely seen in other films.

December 16 - **Canada's** most populous province, Ontario, will impose a new lockdown beginning December 19th for its 14 million inhabitants, its premier announced December 14th as Covid-19 cases climb.

"Make no mistake, thousands of lives are at stake right now. If we fail to take action now the consequences could be catastrophic," Premier Doug Ford said at a news conference. Ford said the lockdown will last 28 days in the southern part of the province and 14 days in the less populated north.

Ford also called on all Ontarians to stay in their homes and only go out when absolutely necessary. Toronto, the country's biggest city, has already been in lockdown for nearly a month. The new restrictions prohibit, among other things, private indoor gatherings outside the family circle. Restaurants and non-essential businesses will only be open for take-away orders or deliveries.

"Unfortunately, despite the restrictions, we've seen growing numbers of people travelling between regions within Ontario," he said, adding that "Our hospitals are filling up more each day."

With the announcement, nearly two-thirds of Canadians will be under full or partial lockdown. Quebec, the country's second most populous province, has put similar measures in effect until January 11.

Canada has recorded more than half a million cases of coronavirus and nearly 14,300 deaths since the pandemic began.

Ontario, the province second most affected by the pandemic after Quebec, has recorded more than 158,000 cases and some 4,200 deaths.

Canada began vaccinating people in high-risk categories - including frontline health care workers and residents and staff of long-term care facilities - on December 14, with a relatively limited supply of the Pfizer-BioNTech vaccine.

December 18 - Today **Sweden** introduced its toughest measures yet in the face of soaring COVID-19 infections, including a recommendation to wear masks at peak hours on public transport, but stopped short of ordering a general lockdown of society.

Prime Minister Stefan Lofven said that non-essential public workplaces, such as municipality gyms, pools and libraries, would close until Jan. 24.

He also said the government now recommended wearing masks on public transport during peak hours, when it is harder for passengers to keep apart.

The government has asked citizens to limit social gatherings to eight people but there are no penalties for breaking the recommendations and Lofven said he still didn't think a lockdown was right.

With a total number of deaths close to 8,000, Sweden's death rate per capita is several times higher than that of its Nordic neighbours but lower than several European countries that opted for lockdowns, such as Britain, Spain, France and Belgium, and in a rare comment on public affairs, Sweden's king said earlier this week the country had failed in its handling of COVID-19.

December 20 – **Wuhan** – In the first week of January of 2021 an international team of ten experts are due to travel to Wuhan China to probe the animal origins of COVID-19. The questions of where the virus came from and how it first crossed over from animals to humans remain a mystery.

December 23 - **London's** Covid-19 crisis is spiralling increasingly out of control with more than 47,000 confirmed cases in a week, official figures reveal - the number of cases in the city more than doubling in a week.

The north east of the capital is the worst hotspot but cases are rising fastest in many inner London boroughs, as well as in Richmond, less than 48 hours after the capital was slammed into emergency Tier 4 strict restrictions.

Health chiefs believe more than 60 per cent of the new cases in London are the VUi202012/01 mutant new strain of coronavirus which is suspected of spreading up to 70 per cent faster.

– **UK** – In a report by Ross Clark of the Daily Mail, he identifies statistics about the pandemic that he says you won't hear from ministers.

"Britain has an elderly population compared with many countries and large numbers of people die every day. In England and Wales in 2019, for example, 530,841 people died – an average of 1,454 every day and this was before the pandemic. While Covid-19 is a serious disease, many of those who have died from it were close to the end of their lives. If it hadn't been Covid-19, it might have been another infectious disease – flu or pneumonia – which dealt the final blow.

Covid has killed some 'healthy' people who did not have underlying conditions, but it has done so in relatively small numbers. Until 4:00 pm today, 47,750 people had died of Covid-19 in English hospitals, but fewer than 2,000 of these had no pre-existing medical condition."

December 29 - **UK** - The United Kingdom is 'back in the eye of the storm' of the coronavirus pandemic according to England's health services chief, with the UK registering a new daily record of 53,135 COVID-19 cases today. The previous record was 41,385 new cases, which occurred yesterday. The large number also reflects a lag due to Christmas reporting of figures, and how a new variant of the virus is spreading across the UK.

The latest government figures also included a further 414 people who died within 28 days of a positive COVID-19 test, which takes the total death toll in the UK to 71,567.

Government advisers say 'decisive action' is needed to prevent a 'catastrophe' next year. Medical staff are being overwhelmed with the numbers of cases.

"We are continuing to see unprecedented levels of COVID-19 infection across the UK, which is of extreme concern particularly as our hospitals are at their most vulnerable," Susan Hopkins, a senior medical advisor to Public Health England, said in a statement.

"It is essential, now more than ever, that we continue to work together to stop the spread of the virus, bring the rate of infection down, and protect the most vulnerable and the NHS [National Health Service]," she said.

Earlier this month Britain became the first country in the world to roll out the vaccine made by Pfizer and BioNTech, and since then more than 600,000 people have received the first dose of the vaccine.

December 31 – **China** - More than 4.43 per cent of 11 million residents in Wuhan - where COVID-19 was first detected - may have been infected with the virus. A new serological study of 34,000 residents from Wuhan and other Chinese cities was done by the Chinese Centre of Disease Control and Prevention (CDC).

The post said the study was conducted one month after China successfully controlled the epidemic earlier this year but did not specify which month.

Several mainstream international media outlets including the BBC and New York Times calculated that based on Wuhan's population of 11.2 million people, nearly 500,000 people may have contracted COVID-19.

This figure would be 10 times the official count of 50,000 confirmed cases reported by the Wuhan Municipal Health Commission, not including asymptomatic cases.

Terry Nolan, who is the Doherty Institute's head of vaccine and immunisation research group in Melbourne said, "The fundamental thing that underlies the suspicion [of China] is that the numbers are being manipulated for some greater political purpose. That's something I'm very sceptical about."

At the height of Wuhan's epidemic in February, Matthew Kavanagh, a specialist in global health and political science at Washington's Georgetown University, wrote "Healthcare workers suspected an outbreak in early December 2019, but information with which the public might have taken preventive measures was suppressed, and communication channels that might have alerted senior officials to the growing threat were shut down."

"Police detained a clinician and seven other people posting reports on 2019-nCoV, threatening punishment for spreading so-called 'rumours.'"

While China appears to have COVID-19 numbers under control, it has continued to punish those who first blew the whistle about the virus, including a citizen-journalist who first reported on the Wuhan outbreak and was handed a four-year jail term this week.

- A poll at the end of 2020 found that only 40% of French people plan to get inoculated.

January 5 – **UK** - Prime Minister Boris Johnson announced a national lockdown for England last night that will likely last through mid-February as the virus continues to ravage the country.

"It is a race, and this variant has made the whole challenge more formidable," said Eric Topol, director of the Scripps Research

Translational Institute in La Jolla, California. "Whatever we saw in 2020 in terms of a challenging virus, it's going to be taken to a new level."

January 6 - Shijiazhuang, the capital of northern **China's** Hebei Province which surrounds Beijing, detected 11 local infections and 30 patients with no symptoms on January 4 - the first time the region has registered native cases in over six months. It has locked down all residential compounds, shut schools and banned public gatherings after reporting 41 COVID-19 cases, according to authorities.

The city, situated 180 miles south-west of Beijing, will start testing the entire population for the coronavirus from today to prevent the spread of the disease, a spokesperson for the local government said.

The emergency measures were announced after the entire Hebei Province entered 'wartime mode' earlier today in response to the health crisis.

Xingtai, a prefecture-level city nearly 80 miles south of Shijiazhuang, has also stepped up its restrictions after three residents tested positive on Monday.

Feng Zijian, deputy director of the Chinese Center for Disease Control (CDC) and Prevention, told state TV on January 5 that the outbreak was likely sparked by a virus strain 'imported from Europe,' but did not provide further details.

Hebei reported 19 local infections and 43 asymptomatic cases between January 2 and January 4, according to data from the provincial health commission. The last time the province recorded locally transmitted infections was in June 2020.

- The **UK** has recorded its highest number of COVID-related deaths since 21 April, and the highest daily increase in cases.

The government figures reported this afternoon showed another 1,041 people have died within 28 days of testing positive for the virus. This is the 10th time since the pandemic began that the daily number of deaths has been above 1,000. As of January 5, 2,645 hospital patients were on ventilators.

The figure was a significant increase from the 830 deaths reported on January 5th, with both days likely to contain some deaths that took place over the Christmas and New Year period that have only just been reported.

There were also another 62,322 new cases reported, an increase from January 5, 60,916 cases. It brings the total number of test-confirmed cases in the UK to 2,836,801.

It was also reported that the number of COVID patients in UK hospital, as of Monday 4 January, for the first time - reaching 30,451. This includes 26,626 patients in England, 1,966 in Wales, 1,282 in Scotland and 577 in Northern Ireland.

January 9 - The positive developments in the race to inoculate the public came as Britain recorded its highest daily number of Covid cases and deaths to date - with 1,325 new fatalities and 68,053 infections confirmed overnight.

- **China** - More than three-quarters of people hospitalised with COVID-19 still suffered from at least one symptom after six months. The research, published in the Lancet medical journal and involving hundreds of patients in the Chinese city of Wuhan, is among the few to trace long-term symptoms of the infection.

January 13 – **UK** – 1,564 deaths in 24 hours. New morgues were being opened.

January 15 - The world passed 2 million coronavirus deaths today, a stunning toll that is continuing to rise as more contagious variants of the virus take hold. The United States has had, by far, the most deaths and cases of any country in the world, at more than 390,000 fatalities, according to Johns Hopkins University. Brazil, India, Mexico, and the United Kingdom follow.

- **Vaccine passports**, which would allow people with immunity to Covid to prove they were at low risk of spreading the disease, are being investigated by companies and countries around the world. But the proposals have also raised fears among critics that they could underpin an oppressive digital ID system and put sensitive medical records in the hands of authorities and employers.

Despite the name, a vaccine passport is not a piece of paper; instead, in the most developed versions of the idea, it is an app or similar system that can prove the bearer has been vaccinated, tested positive for Covid antibodies, or recently received a negative test.

There would be no need to build and operate a privacy violating centralised database.

The pressures on such a system are similar to those faced by the NHS in building its contact-tracing app. A centralised system, which simply keeps a database of people who have been vaccinated and allows them to grant access to others, may be easiest to build, but poses unacceptable privacy burdens. Instead, one proposed system, developed by two British firms, Mvine and iProov, would be secured with a biometric identifier, preventing the records from being accessed without the bearer's consent.

– **UK** - Is the new strain spreading differently? Mr. Johnson said today, " Please remember that this disease can be passed on not just by standing too near someone in a supermarket queue, but also by handling something touched by an infected person. And remember also that one in three people with Covid have no symptoms, and that is why that original message of hands, face and space, washing your hands, is as important now as it has ever been."

January 21 - **Beijing**'s city government has strengthened quarantine rules for overseas travellers after the country recorded more than 100 new cases every day over the past week.

Chinese state media Xinhua reported Beijing authorities announcing at a press conference on Tuesday that foreigners would have to undertake "14+7+7" health management measures after they landed in the city. This included 14 days of hotel quarantine, followed by seven days of home quarantine, and a seven-day health monitoring period where they could not attend public gatherings. Previously, travellers did not have to undertake the extra seven-day health monitoring period.

Beijing said it would investigate all individuals who entered the city from abroad from December 10 and shut down a subway station after reporting the biggest daily jump in new COVID-19 cases in more than three weeks.

The measures come amid what has become the country's most severe COVID-19 outbreak since March 2020. It is also ahead of the key Chinese Lunar New Year holiday season in February, when hundreds of millions travel, raising fear another major COVID-19 wave could bring the country back into a debilitating standstill.

The tighter quarantine rules came after sustained high numbers of new daily cases, with the country recording a total of 103 new COVID-19 cases on January 19 (local time), down from 118 a day earlier, according to the National Health Commission.

North-eastern Jilin province reported 46 new cases, however, setting another record in daily cases, while Hebei province surrounding Beijing reported 19 new cases. Beijing reported seven new cases, matching the total reported on December 28.

The total number of confirmed COVID-19 cases in mainland China now stands at 88,557, while the death toll remained unchanged at 4,635.

The figures exclude cases reported in Hong Kong and Macau, which are Chinese territories but independently report their data.

January 23 – **UK** - Mr. Johnson said that the new strain may in fact be more deadly. "[It] may be associated with a higher degree of mortality," he told a Downing Street press conference. But there remain plenty of unknowns.

The new strain of coronavirus, which was first publicly identified in December 2020 in the south east of England, primarily in Kent and Essex, has now spread rapidly across the country to become the dominant strain.

Chris Witty and other medical experts informed the WHO of the existence of the new strain - which was believed to have first been noticed in lab testing back in September or October - highlighting that it seemed to transmit faster than the previous one (Mr. Johnson estimated it was up to 70% more transmissible).

Despite its speed, the government was quick to reassure people that it was not more deadly, nor would it require a different course of treatment. It could also still be targeted by the vaccine programme.

Although the strain was initially localised, it spread quickly and by January was the most common form in England and Northern Ireland and has spread internationally. It was also credited for driving the number up prior to Christmas, the increased death toll, and rising pressure on the NHS and ICU capacity.

The government has not issued a different list of symptoms for the new strain and reiterates the three official symptoms that already exist: a fever (high temperature), a new and persistent cough, and a loss or change to your sense of taste or smell.

January 27 – **UK** - A survey by the Office for National Statistics (ONS), found that coughs, sore throats and fatigue are more common in people with the new strain. A loss of taste or sense of smell is less likely in those with the new strain. There was no evidence of difference in the percentages reporting gastrointestinal symptoms."

January 31 - **UK** declares double victory in coronavirus fight. Victory No.1 came in Europe's outrageous vaccine war as the EU admitted they had made a mistake about vaccines being returned. Cabinet Office boss Michael Gove announced the retreat by Brussels with the words: "The European Union has stepped back."

Victory No.2 came as a top scientist announced that Britain's massive vaccine roll-out – which today included vaccines at Newmarket racecourse – appears to be reducing infections. Professor Anthony Harnden said the latest data shows a single vaccine is effective in protecting both over-80s and young adults.

Virologist Dr. Chris Smith said the vaccine rollout would only 'start to put a barrier in the way of the virus' by 'mid-to-late February.' Dr. Smith said: "Yes we're making enormous strides, and yes, we're getting the vaccine into lots of people, but we won't expect to see it really begin to bite, I would say, for a few more weeks yet because as those numbers climb, and as people's immunity builds, that's when we're really going to start to put a barrier in the way of the virus."

Since the Pfizer-BioNTech vaccine was first rolled out in early December, some 7.7 million people have received their first vaccine, indicating the NHS is more than halfway towards its target of vaccinating 15 million in the four most vulnerable groups by the middle of February.

– **Wuhan, China** - Hundreds of pages of information connected to studies carried out by the top-secret Wuhan Institute of Virology were wiped alongside key data from a top virologist, Shi Zhengli, nicknamed "Batwoman." The 56-year-old earned the nickname for her research gathering samples in bat caves.

More than 300 studies published by the National Natural Science Foundation of China - including investigations into diseases that transfer from animals to humans - are no longer available. The mass removal of the online studies has reaffirmed fears that China is trying to hamper the investigation into the origin of COVID-19.

Data, including the risk of cross-species infection from bats with Sars-like coronaviruses and investigations into human pathogens carried by bats have been wiped - key sources for the inquiry into the origin of coronavirus.

Iain Duncan Smith, former Conservative leader and member of the International Parliamentary Alliance on China said: "China is clearly trying to hide the evidence. It is vital that there is a thorough investigation into what happened, but China seems to be doing all it can to stop that happening."

Stories regarding the 'cover-up' have continued to swirl in the wake of World Health Organisation investigators being blocked from entering the country. The extraordinary turn of events sparked international outrage as China was plagued with accusations of fudging numbers of cases and death tolls, as reports of whistle blowers talking to US authorities continue.

February 1 – Controls are being stepped up in parts of the **UK** hit by new strains of COVID-19. Virologist Julian Tang, of the University of Leicester, said, "E484K was thought to be the main mutation impacting on vaccine efficacy," adding that its emergence in different strains of the disease was 'worrying.' Failure to impose control on the circulation of the virus could lead to the UK becoming a 'melting pot' for new mutations, he warned.

The cases in Liverpool and the Bristol area were made public as door-to-door testing began in eight other postcode areas to stem the spread of the South African coronavirus variant.

Eleven cases in and around Bristol have been identified as the variant which originally emerged in Kent, with the addition of the E484K mutation found in the South African strain. And a cluster of 32 cases in Liverpool showed the same mutation to the original strain of coronavirus which arrived in the UK around a year ago.

January 5 – The 2020 **Tokyo** Olympics had to be cancelled because of COVID-19, and the future of the 2021 Olympics has been thrown into doubt after a report surfaced suggesting the Japanese government has concluded the coronavirus pandemic will force the event to be cancelled. But John Coates, the Australian Olympic Committee president, and International Olympic Committee vice-president, said preparations for the Tokyo Games were 'proceeding fully,' saying there had been no discussion among organisers about another postponement or cancellation.

The Australian Olympic Committee is continuing its planning to ensuring the Australian Olympic Team arrives in Tokyo, competes, and returns home safe and COVID-free.

- **Islamabad, Pakistan** – "Pakistani military aircraft carrying the first doses of the coronavirus vaccine landed in the Pakistani capital Islamabad early today," Dr Faisal Sultan said. China donated half a million doses of Sinopharm vaccine to the country.

Sinopharm, a Chinese state-owned company, has developed one of two major Chinese vaccines to have been rolled out around the globe, alongside Sinovac's Coronavac vaccine.

Phase three trials for the Chinese CanSino vaccine are also ongoing in Pakistan, which granted emergency use authorisation for the Sinopharm, AstraZeneca and Sputnik V vaccines last month.

The Sinopharm shipment marks the first vaccines to be imported into the South Asian country of 220 million people, where more than 546,000 cases of the coronavirus have been registered since the pandemic began. At least 11,785 people have died from the virus, with daily case numbers at an average of 1,800 over the last two weeks, according to official data.

The first doses of the vaccine will be provided to more than 400,000 front-line healthcare workers across the country, as per the government's vaccine roll-out plan. After that, the shots will be provided to citizens over the age of 65, who generally face a higher mortality risk from the virus.

February 9 - The **European Union** has finalised a deal with Pfizer and BioNTech for the supply of an additional 300 million doses of their COVID-19 vaccine, a European Commission spokesman told Reuters on Monday.

- In **South Africa**, where another variant strain - 501Y.V2 - is spreading rapidly, the government has taken the extraordinary step of backing out from the Oxford-AstraZeneca vaccine. Although public health experts think the vaccine is still successful at preventing more serious cases of 501Y.V2, the government says that the Oxford-AstraZeneca vaccine doesn't provide protection against mild cases.

How should you prepare for having the vaccination?

Even if you're far down the list - it's important to know what to do before you roll up your sleeve - from how to make the most of the shot, to how to prepare for the possible side effects.

Don't buy into immune-boosting hacks. Some companies are advertising vitamin regimens to strengthen the immune system and boost protection from the vaccine, but there's no data to suggest any benefits from them.

"People do not need to try to find immune boosting supplements in order to make the vaccine work," says Jeanne Noble, the director of COVID response for the Emergency Department at the University of California, San Francisco. "The new mRNA vaccines are among the most highly effective we have."

Avoiding alcohol and getting a good night's sleep, may be useful but for different reasons. Poor sleep can lead to fatigue or headaches, which if someone at the vaccination site believes they are COVID symptoms, might result in them turning you away. Finally, you may want to leave the toasts to after your second dose, as some of the vaccine's side effects can make a dreadful hangover – even worse.

"Pregnant women can and should get vaccinated. Others need to be careful if they're prone to serious allergic reactions. Most people with allergies (even those with bad reactions to eggs) shouldn't be particularly concerned about getting the COVID-19 vaccine," Noble says. "But if you have ever experienced anaphylaxis - a serious response that throws the body into shock after exposure to an allergen - you should take special precautions.

Keep taking your allergy medications as your doctor prescribed, and if you have an EpiPen, bring it to your appointment just in case. In the hours before you leave home, avoid anything that might increase your chance of having an allergic reaction, such as exposure to cold air. At the vaccine site, tell the doctor or nurse in charge about your condition so they can take precautions if necessary.

Even though allergic reactions to the vaccine are rare, medical protocol forces people to stay at the site for 15 minutes after getting the shot to make sure there's no negative response. But if you have a history of anaphylaxis, healthcare workers in charge will ask you to wait for 30 minutes before you leave, so it's a good idea to bring a fully charged phone or something else to occupy yourself.

The vaccine against the novel coronavirus has quickly become infamous for causing pain at the injection site. Unfortunately, there's no way to prevent this, but getting the shot in your non-dominant arm can mean less discomfort the following day, which you can then treat with a warm compress."

Mild headaches and body aches are relatively common, and while more than half of the people who have received the vaccine report feeling fatigued after the first dose," Noble says, "Only about 1 in 10 patients will run a fever, so chances are you won't need to stay away from work.

Still, no one likes to deal with a sore arm and an annoying headache for an entire day, so you might be tempted to take preventative painkillers before getting the vaccine. Don't do it, though, and leave any pain medication for after you get your shot.

The second dose of the COVID-19 vaccine is more likely to cause side effects, but just as with the first one, don't premedicate. Instead, before you leave for your appointment, make sure to leave medications at hand at home in case you need them afterwards. No one wants to go fishing for a warm compress when their arm hurts."

February 7 – **New York** – Live Science have identified that the coronavirus that causes COVID-19 can infiltrate star-shaped cells in the brain, setting off a chain reaction that may disable and even kill nearby neurons, according to a new study. The star-shaped cells, called astrocytes, perform many roles in the nervous system and provide fuel to neurons, which transmit signals throughout the body and brain. In a lab dish, the study found that infected astrocytes stopped producing critical fuel for neurons and secreted an 'unidentified' substance that poisoned nearby neurons.

If infected, astrocytes do the same in the brain, that could explain some of the structural changes seen in patients' brains, as well as some of the 'brain fog' and psychiatric issues that seem to accompany some cases of COVID-19, the authors wrote.

That said, the new study, to the preprint database medRxiv, has not been peer-reviewed yet, and an expert told Live Science that 'this is very preliminary data' that still needs to be verified with additional research, especially regarding to the neuron death seen in lab dishes.

February 9 - **Wuhan, China** - The coronavirus is unlikely to have leaked from a Chinese lab and is more likely to have jumped to humans from an animal, a World Health Organization team has concluded, as the group wrapped up a visit to explore the origins of the virus.

The Wuhan Institute of Virology in central China has collected extensive virus samples, leading to allegations that it may have caused the original outbreak by leaking the virus into the surrounding community. China has strongly rejected that possibility and has promoted other theories for the virus's origins. The WHO team that visited Wuhan, where the first cases of COVID-19 were discovered in December 2019, is considering several theories for how the disease first ended up in humans.

"Our initial findings suggest that the introduction through an intermediary host species is the most likely pathway and one that will require more studies and more specific targeted research," WHO food safety and animal diseases expert Peter Ben Embarek said at a news conference today.

"However, the findings suggest that the laboratory incidents hypothesis is extremely unlikely to explain the introduction of the virus to the human population and will not be suggested as an avenue of future study," said Embarek.

The WHO team's mission is intended to be an initial step delving into the origins of the virus, which is believed to have originated in bats before being passed to humans through another species of wild animal, such as a pangolin or bamboo rat, which is considered an exotic delicacy by some in China. "Transmission through the trade in frozen products was also a possibility," Embarek added.

– **UK** - People who have received their Covid vaccine could be given scannable QR codes allowing them to leave the country in 'passport' schemes being funded by the taxpayer. Details of two ventures developing ways for Britons to confirm they have had the vaccines were shared with The Telegraph yesterday.

Logifect, a firm handed £62,000 in grants by the agency InnovateUK, has designed a phone app, due to launch next month, that allows Britons to show confirmation of their vaccinations that will be especially useful when people travel.

iProov and Mvine, two companies given a £75,000 grant for their joint drive, are working on digital 'certificates' that would allow people to prove their immunity when asked.

Executives behind the first drive said they planned to reach out to Government officials in the hope their technologies can help with reopening after the lockdown.

Publicly, ministers have been cautious about endorsing calls for vaccines 'passports,' warning that such a move could be discriminatory. However, privately the position inside the Government is much more nuanced, with multiple ministers believing some form of system allowing people to show they have had vaccines is likely.

Government insiders told The Telegraph that officials were already investigating numerous options for vaccine passports in the context of allowing for international travel.

February 14 – A **Queensland** inventor, Anna Ballantyne, has invented pop-up isolation rooms (Redirooms) that are compact and transportable tents which help prevent the spread of COVID-19 and other common contact and droplet pathogens. In eight months, the inventor with help from husband Justin, has chalked up $10 million worth of sales in eight months.

UK's National Health Service have purchased them with one being deployed every 40 minutes. The rooms can be set up in any hospital wing and remove the need for permanent isolation rooms. They are being marketed in Spain, Israel and Romania with plans to launch in the US this May.

– **France** - A 58-year-old man with a history of asthma was initially tested positive for COVID-19 in September. He recovered and tested negative in December but was re-admitted to hospital in January with the South African variant and is in critical condition on a ventilator.

February 15 - **New Zealand** authorities have implemented a 72-hour lockdown on Auckland after three mystery coronavirus cases were detected in the city.

Under the lockdown, residents will only be allowed to leave home for shopping and essential work purposes. The new infections prompted a halt in quarantine-free travel between New Zealand and Australia, with Kiwi flights now classified as red zone flights for an initial 72-hour period.

World Leaders:

The countries most affected by coronavirus are the USA, Brazil, Russia, Spain, the United Kingdom, Italy and France. Here are the photos of their leaders:

The countries that are recognized as having managed the crisis best are Germany, Taiwan, New Zealand, Iceland, Finland, Norway and Denmark. Here are the photos of their leaders:

[Did you notice the fifference in the leaders?]

February 17 - Some top **UK** firms plan to make COVID-19 vaccinations mandatory for staff through 'no jab, no job' employment contracts, The Financial Times reported.

Law firms that declined to be named told the FT that businesses, ranging from care-home operators to big multinationals, were considering contracts that require new and current employees to get a vaccine as soon as it is offered to the UK's adult population.

Pimlico Plumbers, which employs more than 400 people, announced in January a 'no jab, no job' policy for new staff members. A spokesperson for the company told Insider that, "Vaccines are a way out and we have to use them as much as possible."

Barchester Healthcare, which owns more than 200 care homes in the country, has said it won't hire new staff who refuse to get vaccinated on non-medical grounds, the FT reported.

"Our long-term ambition is that all patient and resident-facing staff will have the COVID-19 vaccine in order to protect both themselves and the vulnerable residents and patients in our care," a Barchester Healthcare spokesperson told Insider.

February 19 - **Greece** is in talks to allow in vaccinated Britons, in hope of 'semi-normal' summer. Summer holidays in Greece could be on the cards for vaccinated travellers, the tourism minister has said. The Greek government was in 'preliminary discussions' with the UK on the question of allowing vaccinated travellers entry into Greece without being tested for Covid-19 first.

Close to 4 million Britons visit Greece every year, marking Britain as one of the most important inbound tourism markets for the Mediterranean country. Currently, all arrivals into Greece have to present a negative Covid test taken within a 72-hour window, and arrivals from the UK also have to undergo a rapid test on arrival.

February 19 – **Helsinki Finland** - Scientists fear a new 'Finnish' mutation of the coronavirus is going undetected and fuelling the spread of the disease. The discovery was made by Helsinki-based Vita Laboratories who say it's unlikely the variant emerged in Finland, given the country's low rate of coronavirus infection. The Scandinavian country has had 51,595 cases and 723 deaths since the pandemic began.

Dubbed 'Fin-796H' the mutation is different from the strains in South Africa and the United Kingdom, the lab said in a statement.

"Vita Laboratoriot Oy and the Institute of Biotechnology at the University of Helsinki have detected a previously unknown variant of the coronavirus in a sample from southern Finland.

"Mutations in this variant make it difficult to detect in at least one of the WHO-recommended PCR tests. This discovery could have a significant impact on determining the spread of the disease," the laboratory said.

February 21 - The **UK** government today vowed to offer a first coronavirus vaccine dose to every adult by the end of July, as it readied to announce a gradual easing of its third lockdown in England. Prime Minister Boris Johnson, who will outline the lockdown review in parliament tomorrow, said the faster inoculation campaign would seek to offer a first dose to everyone aged over 50 by mid-April. The previous targets were to inoculate over 50s by May, and all adults by September.

"We will now aim to offer a jab to every adult by the end of July, helping us protect the most vulnerable sooner, and take further steps to ease some of the restrictions," Johnson said, while stressing the exit would be 'cautious and phased.'

Britain, one of the hardest-hit countries in the world by the Covid-19 pandemic with more than 120,000 deaths, was also the first nation to begin a mass vaccination campaign, in December. More than 17 million people have now received at least a first dose - one third of the adult UK population.

February 26 – **US** - A new coronavirus variant with concerning mutations is on the rise in New York City, according to news reports. This latest coronavirus variant, dubbed B.1.526, first emerged in New York in November 2020, and it now accounts for about 25% of coronavirus genomes that were sequenced from New York in February and posted to a global database called GISAID, according to The New York Times.

Two 'branche'" or versions of the B.1.526 lineage exist, both with worrisome mutations. One branch has a mutation called E484K, which has also been seen in other coronavirus variants, including those identified in South Africa and Brazil. This mutation may reduce the ability of certain antibodies to neutralize, or inactivate, the virus, and may help the coronavirus partially evade COVID-19 vaccines, Live Science previously reported. The other branch has a mutation called S477N, which may help the virus bind more tightly to cells, the Times reported.

February 27 - **UK** is beating the US in the race to control COVID variants. The tests needed for detecting variants, known as genome sequencing tests, have not been authorized by the US Food and Drug Administration (FDA) as a diagnostic tool, according to Kaiser Health News. Laboratory officials say they cannot tell patients or their physicians if they have been infected with a mutant strain.

This is in stark comparison with the UK's Office for National Statistics, which has very detailed accounts of which regions of England have cases of the variant and what percentage of test are linked to mutant strains.

Wuhan China Investigation results:

February 25 – In a report made by Dominic Dwyer from the University of Sydney he stated: It was in Wuhan, in central China, that the virus, now called SARS-CoV-2, emerged in December 2019, unleashing the greatest infectious disease outbreak since the 1918-19 influenza pandemic.

Our investigations concluded the virus was most likely of animal origin. It probably crossed over to humans from bats, via an as-yet-unknown intermediary animal, at an unknown location. Such "zoonotic" diseases have triggered pandemics before, but we are still working to confirm the exact chain of events that led to the current pandemic. Sampling of bats in Hubei province and wildlife across China has revealed no SARS-CoV-2 to date.

We visited the now-closed Wuhan wet market which, in the early days of the pandemic, was blamed as the source of the virus. Some stalls at the market sold 'domesticated' wildlife products. These are animals raised for food, such as bamboo rats, civets and ferret badgers. There is also evidence some domesticated wildlife may be susceptible to SARS-CoV-2. However, none of the animal products sampled after the market's closure tested positive for SARS-CoV-2.

We also know not all of those first 174 early COVID-19 cases visited the market, including the man who was diagnosed in December 2019 with the earliest onset date.

However, when we visited the closed market, it's easy to see how an infection might have spread there. When it was open, there would have been around 10,000 people visiting a day, in close proximity, with poor ventilation and drainage.

There's also genetic evidence generated during the mission for a transmission cluster there. Viral sequences from several of the market cases were identical, suggesting a transmission cluster. However, there was some diversity in other viral sequences, implying other unknown or unsampled chains of transmission.

A summary of modelling studies of the time to the most recent common ancestor of SARS-CoV-2 sequences estimated the start of the pandemic between mid-November and early December. There are also publications suggesting SARS-CoV-2 circulation in various countries earlier than the first case in Wuhan, although these require confirmation.

CHAPTER 2

STATISTICS DURING DAYS 200 – 400

Near the end of my first book about the coronavirus [Covid-19 200 Days – Facts and Fun] I quoted the following:

Stats related to Covid-19 as of August 9th, 2020:

- Cases:
  - o Italy – 250,566 – up 4,280 in 2 weeks
  - o USA – 4,960,972 – up 734,062
  - o UK – 355,219 – up 55,108
  - o Australia – 21,084 – up 6,149
  - o New Zealand – 1,569 – up 13
  - o Canada – 119,746 – up 5,149
  - o Brazil – 3,035,422 – up 593,047
  - o India – 2,153,010 – up 717,557
  - o Russia – 887,536 – up 69,416

  - o Global – 16,117,308 – up 5,024,126

- Deaths:
  - o Italy – 35,205 – up 93
  - o USA – 151,029 – up 14,112
  - o UK – 46,574 – up 5,208
  - o Australia – 888 – up 727
  - o New Zealand – 22 – up 0
  - o Canada – 8,981 – up 80
  - o Brazil –101,049 – up 13,431
  - o India – 43,379 – up 10,608
  - o Russia – 15,001 – up 1,647

  - o Global – 645,482 – up 119,991

Subsequently the figures rose and rose…

Stats related to Covid-19 as of August 17, 2020:

- Cases:
  - o Italy – 253,915 – up 7,629 in three weeks
  - o USA – 5,485,652 – up 1,258,742

- o UK – 318,484 – up 8,234
- o Australia – 23,288 – up 8,353
- o New Zealand – 1,579 – up 23
- o Canada – 122,087 – up 7,490
- o Brazil – 3,340,197 – up by 897,822
- o India – 2,647,316 – up by 1,211,863
- o Russia – 922,853 – up by 104,733
- o Global – 21,593,607 – up 5,476,299

- Deaths:

  - o Italy – 35,396 – up 284 in 3 weeks
  - o USA – 172,086 – up 35,169
  - o UK – 45,878 – up 4,512
  - o Australia – 396– up 235
  - o New Zealand - 22 – up 0
  - o Canada – 9,026 – up 125
  - o Brazil –107,879 – up 20,261
  - o India – 51,045 – up 18,274
  - o Russia – 15,685 – up 233
  - o Global – 773,649 – up 128,167

Stats related to Covid-19 as of September 1, 2020:

- New Cases today:

  - o Italy – 1,365
  - o USA – 3,824
  - o UK – **** (no figures found)
  - o Australia – 123
  - o New Zealand – 2
  - o Canada – 315
  - o Brazil – 16,158
  - o India – 78,761
  - o Russia – 4,980
  - o Global – **** (no figures found)

- Cases:

  - o Italy – 268,218 – up 21,932 in five weeks
  - o USA – 6,081,372– up 1,854,462
  - o UK – 334,467 – up 34n356

- o   Australia – 25,746 – up 10,811
- o   New Zealand – 1,738 – up 182
- o   Canada – 128,054 – up 13,457
- o   Brazil – 3,862,311 – up by 1,419,936
- o   India – 3,681,073 – up by 2,245,620
- o   Russia – 995,319 – up by 177,199
- o   Global – 25,051,178 – up 8,933,870

- Deaths:

  - o   Italy – 35,112 – up 365 in five weeks
  - o   USA – 185,870 – up 48,953
  - o   UK – 41,499 – up 133
  - o   Australia – 652 – up 491
  - o   New Zealand - 22 – up 0
  - o   Canada – 9,118 – up 217
  - o   Brazil – 120,828 – up 33,210
  - o   India – 65,427 – up 32,656 (double what it was on July 27th)
  - o   Russia – 17,176 – up 3,822
  - o   Global – 843,586 – up 198,104

Stats related to Covid-19 as of October 1st, 2020:

- Cases:

  - o   Italy – 246,286 – up 66,843 in seven plus weeks
  - o   USA – 7,137,767 – up 2,176,795
  - o   UK – 460,178 – up 104,959
  - o   Australia – 27,096 – up 6,012
  - o   New Zealand – 1,848 – up 279
  - o   Canada – 160,535 – up 40,789
  - o   Brazil – 4,847,092 – up by 1,811,670
  - o   India – 6,312,584 – up by 4,159,574
  - o   Russia – 1,185,231 – up by 297,695
  - o   Global – 35,011,322

- Deaths:

  - o   Italy – 35,918 – up 713 in seven plus weeks
  - o   USA – 195,641 – up 44,612
  - o   UK – 41,366 – up 4,372
  - o   Australia – 888 – up 593

- o New Zealand - 25 – up 3
- o Canada – 9,319 – up 338
- o Brazil –144,680 – up 43,631
- o India – 98,678 – up 55,299
- o Russia – 20,891 – up 5,960
- o Global – 1,034,865

Stats related to Covid-19 as of November 1st, 2020:

- Cases:

  - o Italy – 679,430 up 433,144 in one month.
  - o USA – 9,194,618 up 2,056,851
  - o UK – 1,011,660 – up 551,482 (more than double in one month)
  - o Australia – 27,590 – up 494
  - o New Zealand – 1,957 – up 109
  - o Canada – 231,999 – up 71,464
  - o Brazil – 5,523,352 – up 676,260
  - o India – 8,182,682 – up 1,870,098
  - o Russia – 1,618,116 – up 432,885
  - o Global – 45,837,788 – up 10,826,466

- Deaths:

  - o Italy – 38,618 up 2,700 in one month.
  - o USA – 233,736 up 38,095
  - o UK – 46,555 up 5,189
  - o Australia – 907 – up 19
  - o New Zealand - 25 – up 0
  - o Canada – 10,110 – up 791
  - o Brazil –159,668 – up 14,988
  - o India – 122,145 – up 23,467
  - o Russia – 27,990 – up 7,099
  - o Global – 1,192,369 – up 157,504

Stats related to Covid-19 as of December 1st, 2020:

- Cases:

  - o Italy – 1,620,901 up 941,471 in one month.
  - o USA – 13,693,774 up 4,499,156
  - o UK – 1,643,086 – up 631,426

- o Australia – 27,912 – up 322
- o New Zealand – 2,050 – up 82
- o Canada – 378,139 – up 146,140
- o Brazil – 6,344,345 – up 820,993
- o India – 9,495,661 – up 1,312,979
- o Russia – 2,322,056 – up 703,940
- o Global – 63,556,040 – up 17,718,252

- Deaths:

  - o Italy – 56,361 up 17,743 in one month.
  - o USA – 271,296 up 37,560
  - o UK – 59,051 up 12,496
  - o Australia – 908– up 1
  - o New Zealand - 25 – up 0
  - o Canada – 12,130 – up 2020
  - o Brazil –173,229 – up 13,561
  - o India – 138,090 – up 12,474
  - o Russia – 27,990 – up 7,099
  - o Global – 1,474,643 – up 282,274

Stats related to Covid-19 as of January 1st, 2021:

- Cases:

  - o Italy – 2,107,1661 up 486,265 in one month.
  - o USA – 19,910,674 up 6,216,900
  - o UK – 1,643,086 – up 631,426
  - o Australia – 28,381 – up 469
  - o New Zealand – 2,262– up 112
  - o Canada – 579,320 – up 201,181
  - o Brazil – 7,619,970 – up 1,275,625
  - o India – 10,285,317 – up 789,656
  - o Russia – 3,159,297 – up 837,241
  - o Global – 82,994,220 – up 19,438,180

- Deaths:

  - o Italy – 74,159 up 17,798 in one month.
  - o USA – 344,877 up 73,581
  - o UK – 73,512 up 14,461
  - o Australia – 909– up 1

- o New Zealand - 25 – up 0
- o Canada – 15,597 – up 3,467
- o Brazil –193,940 – up 20,711
- o India – 138,090 – up 12,474
- o Russia – 57,019 – up 29,029 (more than double of last month)
- o Global – 1,810,360 – up 335,717

Stats related to Covid-19 as of February 1st, 2021:

- • Cases:

  - o Italy – 2,541,783 up 434,617 in one month.
  - o USA – 26,308,290 up 6,397,616
  - o UK – 3,817,176 – up 2,174,090
  - o Australia – 28,811 – up 430
  - o New Zealand – 2,305– up 43
  - o Canada – 775,048 – up 195,728
  - o Brazil – 9,176,975 – up 1,557,005
  - o India – 10,752,872 – up 467,555
  - o Russia – 3,850,439 – up 691,142
  - o Global – 102,791,996 – up 19,797,776

- • Deaths:

  - o Italy – 88,279 up 14,120 in one month.
  - o USA – 443,817 up 98,940
  - o UK – 106,158 up 32,646
  - o Australia – 909– up 0
  - o New Zealand - 25 – up 0
  - o Canada – 19,942– up 4,345
  - o Brazil –223,971 – up 30,031
  - o India – 154,397 – up 16,307
  - o Russia – 73,182 – up 16,163
  - o Global – 2,224,395 – up 414,035

- • *Stats related to Covid-19 as of March 1st, 2021:*

- • Cases:

  - o Italy – 2,925,265 up 383,482 in one month.
  - o USA – 28,833,039 up 2,524,749
  - o UK – 4,176,554 up 359,378

- o Australia – 28,970 upn159
- o New Zealand – 2,376 up 71
- o Canada – 864,196 up 89,148
- o Brazil – 10,517,232 up 1.340,257
- o India – 11,112,056 up 359,184
- o Russia – 4,246,079 up 395,640
- o Global – 113,972,687 up 11,180,083

- Deaths:

- o Italy – 97,699 up 9,420 in one month.
- o USA – 517,204 up 73,387
- o UK – 122,849 up 16,691
- o Australia – 909– up 0
- o New Zealand - 26 – up 1
- o Canada – 21,960 up 2,018
- o Brazil –254,263 up 20,292
- o India – 157,195 up 21,798
- o Russia – 86,112 up 12,930
- o Global – 2,528,535 up 304,140

Increase in Covid-19 cases for last 200 days:

August 1st, 2020	March 1st 2021	Up
Cases:		
Italy – 250,566	2,925,265	2,674,699
USA – 4,960,972	28,833,039	23,872,067
UK – 355,219	4,176,554	3,821,335
Australia – 21,084	28,970	7,886
New Zealand – 1,569	2,376	807
Canada – 119,746	864,196	744,450
Brazil – 3,035,422	10,517,232	7,481,810
India – 2,153,010	11,112,056	8,959,046
Russia – 887,536	4,246,079	3,358,543
Global – 16,117,308	113,972,687	97,855,379
Deaths:		
Italy – 35,205	97,699	62,494
USA – 151,029	517,204	366,175

UK – 46,574	122,849	76,275
Australia – 888	909	21
New Zealand – 22	26	4
Canada – 8,981	21,960	12,979
Brazil –101,049	254,263	153,214
India – 43,379	157,195	113,816
Russia – 15,001	86,112	71,111
Global – 645,482	2,528,535	1,883,053

CHAPTER 3

CLINICAL TRIALS FOR A VACCINE

August 11 – **Russia** – Vladimir Putin stunned the world when he announced the approval of Moscow's Gamaleya Institute of Epidemiology and Microbiology's vaccine. Sputnik 5 – only tested on 76 people. It raises concerns that if it failed or people had adverse reactions, it would be used as propaganda by anti-vax activists. One of Putin's daughters was inoculated in a sign the process was a publicity stunt. It cannot be used until January 1, 2021, leaving time for a stage 3 trial. Philippine's president Rodrigo Duterte has offered to assist and be a guinea pig.

Russia announced approval for a COVID-19 vaccine, and President Vladimir Putin said he wanted to start mass producing it and offering it to healthcare workers. However, Russian vaccine developers have skipped the all-important phase 3 of clinical trials. This means that the vaccine, named Sputnik V, has not been tested for effectiveness or safety on a large scale, and it puts those who will soon be using it at risk.

Once a promising vaccine is developed, there are hurdles it must clear before it can be rolled out. These are:

Preclinical: Testing in animals. Does the vaccine produce antibodies? Does it protect against illness? What dose is necessary?

Phase 1: Testing in a small number of humans. This phase is about making sure the vaccine is safe.

Phase 2: More testing in humans. Does the vaccine work?

Phase 3: Testing in a larger number of humans to confirm its effectiveness.

Then, after it has been rolled out:

Phase 4: Ongoing surveillance to make sure it's safe and doesn't have long-term adverse effects.

No vaccine is 100 per cent safe, and some people experience side effects, particularly those who are immunocompromised, so completion of rigorous clinical trials is paramount.

"Without phase 3, they just cannot have any awareness of the potential pitfalls and determine who should get the vaccine and who shouldn't," said Damian Purcell, laboratory head at the Doherty Institute.

August 15 - CureVad, backed by Microsoft founder and billionaire Bill Gates started an early-stage coronavirus trial in healthy volunteers in June with results expected in the final quarter of this year. The company is hoping to expand with a new manufacturing facility in Germany that is expected to produce billions of vaccine doses.

New Test to prove a person has had COVID-19

August 23 – An announcement was made that a test had been discovered that would reveal whether a person has had COVID-19 and may not have known they were infectious. The Brisbane company Ellume is expanding to create hundreds of jobs and have begun sending their tests for sale in the US who have authorised its use in that country. The new site would be the biggest diagnostics manufacturing facility in Australia and can produce fifteen million tests a month. Australia will require approval from the Therapeutic Goods Administration before making it available in Australia.

August 30 – Dr. Anthony Fauci, said that three vaccines have been set up for testing to deliver 300 million doses by January 2021. He added that he would oppose any attempt to rush through a vaccine for political purposes.

September 12 - The **UK** has ordered a total of 340 million doses of potential coronavirus vaccines from six manufacturers.

The EU has done a deal said to be worth €2.4 billion (£2.2 billion) with one developer, while the US has orders with six companies for 800 million doses under 'Operation Warp Speed,' with options on 1.6 billion more.

Wealthy countries are paying up-front for something that has not yet been proven to work - willing to spend whatever it takes to get their economies running again. And yet they could have backed the wrong horse. It is a lottery on an unprecedented scale.

They cannot know whether the gamble will pay off. Earlier this week, the front-runner the UK and EU have ordered, the Oxford

University-AstraZeneca vaccine, was put on pause after a volunteer became ill. It may not be vaccine-related, but such things can happen.

September 25 - **New York** Governor Andrew Cuomo said yesterday that his state will conduct its own verification of any federally approved vaccination, citing concerns that the vetting process is overly politicized.

"Frankly, I'm not going to trust the federal government's opinion," the Democratic state leader told journalists.

The governor voiced alarm that Trump said earlier this week that the White House 'may or may not' authorize Food and Drug Administration rules tightening standards for vaccine approval.

"That sounds like a political move," Trump said of the FDA plans, which he said could unnecessarily delay the release of a vaccine he has vowed would be available by the November 3rd electoral vote.

Health experts including the nation's top infectious disease official, Dr. Anthony Fauci, have estimated a vaccine could be proven safe by the final months of 2020 - calling Trump's claims that it could be ready before the election into question.

A recent Kaiser Family Foundation poll showed that more than half of US residents said they would not get the vaccine even if it were available for free prior to the presidential election. That lack of trust could ultimately hamper efforts to halt Covid-19's spread, many experts say.

Cuomo also said, "It's increasingly clear that the President and his advisers are trying to undermine the credibility of experts whose facts run counter to the administration's political agenda."

Leading vaccine seekers

England – Oxford University's ChAd0x1 – a chimpanzee adenovirus developed for the Middle Eastern Respiratory Syndrome vaccine. Work started in 2014 on Ebola, repurposed for coronavirus. Currently in Stage 3 trials in the US with 30,000 volunteers, plus Brazil and South African studies. A Stage 2 trial in July, found that it produced antibodies and T-Cell responses in 1,077 people. More than 1.4 billion funding has been pledged.

Australia does not have a contract with Oxford, but talks are at an advanced stage.

USA – Moderna's mRNA-1273. US pharmaceutical company's ground-breaking DNA-based vaccine, which would be the first of this type if it won approval. Stage 3 trials are under way after successful early trials in March. The vaccine has received $672 million from Operation Warp Speed, a public-private partnership in the US. Moderna claims it could produce 1 billion doses per year from 2021, if trials work.

China – Sinovac's Coronavac. Already in Stage 3 trials, but the number of participants in Stage 2 was almost half of those enrolled in the similar Oxford trial. Antibodies were found in volunteers after 14 days. The study in Brazil is under way. It is unlikely that Australia would get access to this vaccine because it would be prioritised for locals first. China's lack of free press raises concerns about the veracity of its claimed success. Scientists in Wuhan Institute of Biological Products are working to fix it. However, like reports about the original infections, the details coming out remain scant.

Australia – The federal government is in the final stages of negotiating with a UK pharmaceutical giant AstraZeneca to produce doses of a vaccine in Australia. It is days away from locking in a deal to produce the vaccine if the trials are successful at combatting the virus. [More later.]

Another **Australian** break-through is already far advanced and COVID-19 patients at Royal Melbourne Hospital will begin testing within weeks if the nasal spray stops the virus by preventing it from moving from the nose and throat to the lungs. If successful, it is also planned to be distributed to frontline health workers to prevent them catching the virus when treating patients. The drug BromAc has been found to dissolve the spike proteins the virus uses to infect human cells. The coronavirus spikes attach to human cells like a lock and key. BromAc dissolves bonds that stabilise the spike. When the bonds break, the spike falls apart. Without spikes the virus can't affect the lungs. Without spikes, the virus won't be able to infect others.

David Morris who works from St. George Hospital in Sydney discovered that when Bromelain was combined with another drug – acetylcysteine, they broke the bonds in the mucus.

August 19 - **Australians** are a step closer to accessing a coronavirus vaccine for free, after the Federal Government secured a major international deal to produce a vaccine frontrunner locally, should trials succeed.

Amid rising pressure to lock in supply of a coronavirus vaccine, the Government has signed an agreement with **UK**-based drug company AstraZeneca to secure the potential COVID-19 vaccine developed by Oxford University, if its trials prove successful.

Prime Minister Scott Morrison said if the vaccine succeeded, the Government would manufacture it immediately and make it free for all Australians.

"The Oxford vaccine is one of the most advanced and promising in the world, and under this deal we have secured early access for every Australian," he said.

The Oxford University vaccine has entered its third phase of trials, where it is tested on thousands of volunteers to confirm its effectiveness.

It means that if the Oxford University vaccine trial succeeds, Australia will receive its vaccine formula straight away and be allowed to manufacture it domestically.

December 2 - The **UK** became the first country in the world to approve the COVID-19 vaccine, paving the way for inoculations to begin next week. Studies show it is 95 per cent effective. It came as Londoners returned to shops, gyms and lidos as they reopened under new Tier 2 restrictions.

Boris Johnson urged the British public not to be 'carried away by over-optimism' following the UK approval of the Pfizer/BioNTech coronavirus vaccine, and he acknowledged there were "immense logistical challenges" in distributing the virus. He added: 'It will inevitably take some months before all the most vulnerable are protected – long, cold months.'

November - **Australia** 1 to 1.5 million health carers and elderly are slated to get the Covid vaccination starting March 2021 subject to national cabinet's approval. This will include doctors, nurses, pharmacists, pathologists, aged care workers and the elderly. The entire Australian population could be vaccinated by the end of 2021. It's likely that two doses of the vaccine will be required – given 30 days apart.

Australians will have access to four types of COVID-19 vaccines. There is hope that they can open their international borders at the end of 2021.

The Pfizer BioNtech mRNA vaccine is leading the global vaccine race. This vaccine uses the virus's genetic code to make a person's own cells produce vaccine antigens and generate immunity. Vaccination will be free, but not compulsory and it is hoped that two-thirds of the population will receive it.

November 20 – **US** - Pfizer Inc. and BioNTech on Friday submitted an application for an emergency use authorization for their trial COVID-19 vaccine candidate, making their vaccine candidate the first in line with U.S. regulators. The two companies had said earlier today that the submission to the Food and Drug Administration was coming.

The companies earlier this week said the vaccine, called BNT162b2, had an efficacy rate of 95% in a late-stage clinical trial. "It is with great pride and joy and even a little relief that I can say that our request for emergency use authorization for our COVID-19 vaccine is now in the FDA's hands," Pfizer Chief Executive Albert Boula said on a company's tweet announcing the development.

The FDA said its advisory committee will meet to discuss the companies' vaccine candidate on December 10. Details will be available next week, it said.

December 8 - The **U.S.** turned down multiple offers from Pfizer to buy more doses of its COVID vaccine, a former head of Pfizer said. Scott Gottlieb, a Pfizer board member who served as the Food and Drug Administration (FDA) commissioner from 2017 – 2019. He told CNBC today that the U.S. appeared to be relying on other vaccine agreements in addition to the 100 million doses of the Pfizer shot that it has ordered at a cost of about $1.95 billion.

Gottlieb said Pfizer had 'gone ahead and entered into agreement with other countries' after their offers were rejected.

Other countries have since secured millions more doses of the Pfizer vaccine. Two days after Pfizer's announcement, the EU revealed that it had secured 200 million doses of the potential vaccine and had requested a further 100 million.

Canada: According to Moderna, it remains on track to be able to deliver up to 56 million doses of the COVID-19 vaccine into the country beginning in 2021. In September, the Canadian government confirmed an order commitment of 20 million doses.

United Kingdom: The U.K. government said it was able to secure access to five million doses of Moderna's mRNA-1273 candidate, which will be enough for about 2.5 million people. Pending safety checks, it could be delivered by Spring next year.

European Union: The European Commission said in August that it would be supplied with 80 million doses of the mRNA-1273 vaccine candidate from Moderna, with an option to purchase up to a further 80 million doses if proven safe and effective.

Switzerland: Moderna confirmed in September that the Swiss Federal Government had agreed to the procurement of 4.5 million vaccine doses of mRNA-1273.

Japan: On October 29, Japan agreed to buy and distribute 50 million doses of the same vaccine.

Middle East: The Israeli government confirmed a future purchase of the candidate. Financial details were unknown. On October 26, the company said a supply agreement was also made with Qatar.

Pfizer/BioNTech

The partnership between U.S. company Pfizer and Germany's BioNTech has resulted in one of the most promising candidates. Today, the firms reiterated they expect to make up to 50 million doses in 2020 and up to 1.3 billion doses by the end of 2021.

United Kingdom: In July, Pfizer/BioNTech said an agreement was reached with the U.K. to supply 30 million doses of the BNT162 mRNA-based candidate. That appears to have since increased to 40 million doses, according to a U.K. government release.

 - A **UK** grandmother has become the first person in the world to be given the Pfizer Covid-19 vaccine as part of a mass vaccination programme. Margaret Keenan, who turns 91 next week, said the injection she received was the 'best early birthday present.'

It was the first of 800,000 doses of the Pfizer/BioNTech vaccine that will be dispensed in the coming weeks. Up to four million more are expected by the end of the month.

Hubs in the UK are starting the rollout by vaccinating the over-80s and some health and care staff.

Japan: On July 31, Pfizer said 120 million doses of the BNT162 mRNA-based vaccine candidate would be supplied to Japan beginning in 2021. As with most deals, the agreement was subject to its clinical success and regulatory approvals.

Canada: Pfizer/BioNTech said in August an agreement with the government of Canada had been reached but did not disclose financial or dosage information.

European Union: On November 11, the European Commission said it had approved a contract with BioNTech and Pfizer settled on an initial purchase of 200 million doses on behalf of all the E.U. States, with an option to request up to a 100 million more.

Australia: Prime Minister Scott Morrison announced in a press release on November 5 that Australia would be supplied with 10 million vaccine doses from Pfizer/BioNTech.

Vaccine Failure

December 11 – **Queensland** - Clinical trials of a COVID-19 vaccine being developed by the University of Queensland in partnership with biotech company CSL have been abandoned after trial participants returned false positive HIV test results.

The vaccine is one of four the Federal Government had committed to purchasing, and agreements had been made to secure 51 million doses of the vaccine.

CSL also said participants were told before the trial started that the vaccine could interfere with certain HIV diagnostic tests.

Federal frontbencher David Littleproud said, "This is why we didn't put all our eggs in one basket, and why we made sure there were four contracts we signed to make sure that we got a vaccine, and this is intrinsically very difficult science.

Release of other vaccines

Australia's CSL began making 30 million doses of AstraZeneca's vaccine last month and the first batch will be ready by Christmas and Australians will get it from March next year.

12 December – The **US** Food and Drug Administration approved the emergency use of Pfizer's COVID- 19 vaccine today as a second wave of coronavirus continue to batter the USA. People could receive the shot as early as December 14 or 15. It is 95% effective in warding off an infection.

This week, two **UK** nurses suffered severe allergic reactions to the Pfizer vaccine, but regulators acted quickly to advise those with anaphylaxis - not to have the vaccine.

Oxford University's Professor Sarah Gilbert who helped develop AstraZenica's vaccine, has urged people to trust the vaccine.

December 16 - **Australia's** COVID-19 vaccine roll-out plan has been revealed, showing who will get it first. But one group of them may not get it at all next year. Children aged under 18 will likely be excluded next year as pharmaceutical companies have not sought regulatory approval for use in younger people yet.

Australians older than 70 will get the vaccine just after 800,000 frontline health workers, aged-care workers and the nation's most vulnerable. Prisoners, other detention inmates and guards will also be among the first because they are deemed to be at greater risk because of crowded conditions.

Those older than 70 will form their own age bracket, the rest of the population will be broken down into 12 five-year age groups that will set out when they receive the vaccine.

 - **Australian** diagnostics company Ellume has won approval from US regulators to sell the first rapid at-home COVID-19 *tests* that don't require a prescription.

The **Brisbane**-based company was granted an emergency use authorisation on Wednesday (AEDT) by the US Food and Drug Administration (FDA) to sell its over-the-counter tests. The company received US$30 million ($40 million AUD) in funding from the US government to develop the tests. Ellume has said it plans to ship over 100,000 tests per day from January, and to deliver 20 million COVID-19 tests to the US within the first half of 2021.

Alongside vaccinations, health experts believe rapid at-home testing will provide a crucial tool to bring the pandemic under control.

"By authorising a test for over-the-counter use, the FDA allows it to be sold in places like drug stores, where a patient can buy it, swab their nose, run the test and find out their results in as little as 20 minutes," Stephen Hahn, the head of the FDA said in a statement.

The US is currently testing around 2 million people a day, but health experts say that figure should be far higher. It can still take several days in many parts of the US to receive a test result.

December 21 - **US** officials including Vice President Mike Pence, House Speaker Nancy Pelosi and Republican Senate Majority Leader Mitch McConnell have been shown getting their vaccinations on live TV. Joe Biden promises to do the same today.

Slovakia's 47-year-old Prime Minister Igor Matovic tested positive after attending a European Union summit. It is believed that French President Emmanuel Macron caught the virus.

China and **Russia** are inoculating using domestically produced vaccines. China reportedly has vaccinated a million people.

The World Health Organisation said vaccines would be distributed early in 2021 to 190 countries.

Brazilian President Jair Bolsonaro has been sceptical of the virus since it first emerged saying it is just a little flu despite 7,213,155 cases and 186,365 of his people dying. Brazil's Supreme Court ruled that the vaccine was obligatory, although could not be forced on people. Their President has refused to have the vaccine.

December 22 – **UK** - Just as vaccines begin to offer hope for a path out of the pandemic, officials in Britain this past weekend sounded an urgent alarm about what they called a highly contagious new variant of the coronavirus circulating in England.

Citing the rapid spread of the virus through London and surrounding areas, Prime Minister Boris Johnson imposed the country's most stringent lockdown since March. "When the virus changes its method of attack, we must change our method of defence," he said.

"The British variant has about 20 mutations, including several that affect how the virus locks onto human cells and infects them. These mutations may allow the variant to replicate and transmit more efficiently," said Muge Cevik, an infectious disease expert at the University of St. Andrews in Scotland and a scientific adviser to the British government.

Train stations in London filled with crowds of people scrambling to leave the city as the restrictions went into effect. On Sunday, European countries began closing their borders to travellers from the United Kingdom, hoping to shut out the new iteration of the pathogen.

In **South Africa**, a similar version of the virus has emerged, sharing one of the mutations seen in the British variant, according to scientists who detected it. That virus has been found in up to 90 percent of the samples whose genetic sequences have been analysed in South Africa since mid-November.

In South Africa, too, scientists were quick to note that human behaviour was driving the epidemic, not necessarily new mutations whose effect on transmissibility had yet to be quantified.

Scientists are worried about these variants but not surprised by them. Researchers have recorded thousands of tiny modifications in the genetic material of the coronavirus as it has hopscotched across the world.

January 26, 2021 - **Johnson and Johnson** will likely publish results from phase three trials of its one-shot coronavirus vaccine next week, the company announced today. Its vaccine is cheaper and easier to store and transport which, along with the fact that it requires just one dose, could help speed the painstakingly slow US vaccine rollout. The 100 million doses Johnson & Johnson has pledged to the US would increase the US supply by about 25 percent.

Vaccinations began five weeks ago, but just 6.2 percent of the US population have had their first doses of either Pfizer's or Moderna's two-dose vaccines. Encouragingly, cases, deaths and hospitalizations were all down last week compared to previous weeks but remains high with an average of 3,287 people dying a day.

Dr. Anthony Fauci said that Johnson & Johnson's vaccine is being tested in both South Africa and Brazil, highly infectious 'super-Covid' variants that scientists fear could evade vaccines.

But even if its results are positive, the FDA is not expected to clear the vaccine for emergency use until March, raising questions over why there must be an agonizing month-long delay.

January 27 - In an interview with the New England Journal of Medicine, Dr. Anthony Fauci said the COVID-19 vaccine rollout must account for the coronavirus' disproportionate impact on people of colour. Black people in the US and the UK have been far more likely than white people to get COVID-19 yet so far, they are receiving vaccines at much lower rates than white people in many states. In 16 US states that have released vaccination data by race, white people are being vaccinated at as much as three times the rates as Black people.

"I think that's the one thing we've really got to be careful of," Fauci said in the interview. "We don't want in the beginning that most of the people who are getting it are otherwise, well, middle-class white people."

January 28 - **Germany** has warned against giving the Oxford-AstraZeneca vaccine to people aged over 65 in a surprise recommendation that will stoke speculation over whether Australia's drug regulator might reach a similar conclusion.

The Standing Committee on Vaccination (STIKO) at Germany's Robert Koch Institute (RKI), the country's main public health authority, found there is insufficient data on the effectiveness of the vaccine, developed by AstraZeneca and the University of Oxford, for this age group, according to a statement from the interior ministry.

"Due to the small number of study participants in the age group 65+ years, no conclusion can be made regarding efficacy and safety in the elderly. This vaccine is therefore currently recommended by STIKO only for persons aged 18-64 years," the panel said in its recommendation.

Responding to the announcement, an AstraZeneca spokesperson said, "Latest analyses of clinical trial data for the AstraZeneca/Oxford Covid-19 vaccine support efficacy in the over

65 years age group." The drug-maker is awaiting a regulatory decision by the European Union medicines regulator, the spokesperson added.

The United Kingdom, whose regulator approved the Oxford/AstraZeneca vaccine nearly a month ago, has been administering doses to people older than 65.

January 30 - **London:** European leaders have given themselves sweeping powers to block crucial coronavirus vaccine shipments to Australia in a ploy condemned as unethical, dangerous, and selfish.

The new export restrictions grant the European Union final say on whether vaccines produced on the continent by pharmaceutical giants Pfizer and AstraZeneca can leave the territory.

The emergency scheme is the latest escalation in a brawl between the EU and two drug firms, which recently warned the number of doses available to Europe over the coming months would be slashed because of production problems.

European leaders retaliated on Friday by publishing new export controls designed to give EU citizens priority access to locally produced vaccines even though other countries, including Australia, are also relying on supplies from European factories.

The EU exempted more than 120 countries from the controls, but Australia did not make the list. EU officials said the export controls would not apply to shipments bound for poor countries or its closest neighbours, although the UK was also not given an exemption.

Pfizer has been exploring whether some or all of Australia's 10 million doses could be made in the United States instead of Europe, should the situation there deteriorate.

Brussels suspects vials produced in Europe have been sent to the UK at the expense of the EU but has offered no evidence to support this claim. The EU has demanded access to tens of millions of doses manufactured in Britain to make up for its expected shortfall over the coming weeks.

- **US** - Doctors are recommending that people should not take over-the-counter pain medications before receiving a coronavirus vaccine. Both the Moderna and Pfizer-BioNTech shots have been known to cause side effects such as pain at the site of injection, headaches, fever, chills and fatigue. Because of this, some people may try to prevent them by taking pain relievers like ibuprofen (Motrin and Advil) or acetaminophen (Tylenol) in advance.

February 1 - The **UK** Government has ordered an extra 40 million doses of Valneva's coronavirus vaccine, taking its total to 100 million doses. The original order of 60 million doses isn't expected to be delivered until the second half of 2021. But the new order won't be delivered until 2022.

It's likely that most or all adults in Britain will already have had one of the other Covid vaccines by the time this one is ready. But infectious disease experts say people may need re-vaccinating in future - like what happens against the flu each winter - and the UK may also export to other countries.

Britain has now ordered a total of 407 million doses of Covid vaccines – enough to give the entire population, including children, six doses each.

Business Secretary Kwasi Kwarteng claimed the stockpile was enough to 'protect the British public in 2021 and beyond.'

Valneva's two-dose vaccine - which is already being manufactured in Scotland - is the first of its kind to be developed in the West and is an 'inactivated whole virus vaccine,' meaning it works by injecting people with a destroyed version of the real coronavirus. This allows the immune system to train itself to attack the actual virus, without the risk of it causing an infection.

– **Canada** - Novavax Inc. has submitted its COVID-19 vaccine candidate to the Canadian health regulator for emergency-use authorization after the pharmaceutical company said last week its vaccine was 89% effective in a UK trial. Novavax has an agreement with the Government of Canada to supply up to 76 million doses of its vaccine.

The vaccine candidate will be reviewed in real-time once the Canadian government accepts the application, which was submitted by the company on January 29, according to a notice on Health Canada's website.

February 2 - **France** - The AstraZeneca COVID-19 vaccine, which was approved by the European Commission last week, will start arriving in France next week at the latest, French European Affairs Minister Clement Beaune said on Monday.

France has so far approved vaccines developed by both Pfizer/BioNTech and Moderna.

- **Mexico**'s Deputy Health Minister Hugo Lopez-Gatell said the Latin American nation had signed a contract for 7.4 million doses of the Russia's Sputnik V vaccine and would likely issue an emergency use authorization for it within hours. More doses are due to arrive in May. Sputnik V was 91.6% effective in preventing people from developing COVID-19.

Mexico has also struck an agreement for 2 million vaccines produced by Serum Institute of India, the world's largest vaccine producer by volume, in February and March, Mexico's Foreign Minister Marcelo Ebrard said.

- **Washington:** The **Biden** administration has signed a $US230 million deal with Australian firm Ellume to dramatically ramp up the production and distribution of rapid at-home COVID-19 tests in the US. The funding is expected to help increase the number of tests that the company can manufacture in the U.S., with a goal of producing 640,000 tests per day by the end of this year.

The deal between Ellume, the Department of Defence and the Department of Health and Human Services includes the purchase of 8.5 million COVID-19 tests that will be distributed across America.

In December Ellume became the first company to win approval from US regulators to sell rapid at-home COVID-19 tests that don't require a prescription.

Andy Slavitt, a senior adviser to the White House COVID-19 response team, said that the Brisbane-based company is expected to produce 19 million tests a month by the end of the year.

Slavitt said the deal was an important step towards mass testing and a lowering of prices. "There's a chicken-and-egg problem, which we have taken a step to solve today," he said.

Ellume's test is expected to cost around US$30 and deliver results in around 20 minutes. To use the test, a person uses a nasal swab and inserts their sample into a digital analyser that comes with the product. Their COVID-19 results are then transmitted to their smartphone via Bluetooth.

Sean Parsons, Ellume's founder and chief executive, said the product would be available over the counter at pharmacies or online. "It's not dissimilar to how the home pregnancy testing works," he said after the deal was announced.

Ellume will retain and improve its production capacity in Australia. But it will also build another larger production facility in the US – a bigger one, to be able to supply these diagnostic products to the American market," Dr. Parsons said. "Our focus is really solely on the US market… Ellume has no products currently for sale in Australia."

- Michael Osterholm, who served on President Joe Biden's coronavirus advisory transition board, said on January 31 that a 'hurricane' was on the way, as he warned about an anticipated surge in cases by spring, "We are going to see something like we have not seen yet in this country."

He went on to say that the Biden administration should start widely offering vaccinations with single doses to reduce the UK variant's spread, with those over 65 years-old a priority for the shots.

Among the concerns expressed by the top epidemiologist was the UK variant, which could be more contagious – and may potentially be more deadly - by as much as 30 per cent.

Currently, there are two vaccines against Covid approved by the US Food and drug Administration, produced by pharmaceutical companies Pfizer and Moderna. Both require two shots, several weeks apart.

 - **Russia -** Scientists gave Sputnik V vaccine the green light today saying it was almost 92% effective in fighting COVID-19 based on peer-reviewed late-stage trial results published in The Lancet international medical journal.

There were 2,144 volunteers over 60 in the Sputnik V trial and the shot was shown to be 91.8% effective when tested on this older group, with no serious side-effects reported that could be associated with the vaccine, The Lancet summary said.

Experts said the Phase III trial results meant the world had another effective weapon to fight the deadly pandemic and justified to some extent Moscow's decision to roll out the vaccine before final data had been released.

Sputnik V has been approved by 15 countries, including Argentina, Hungary and the United Arab Emirates and this will rise to 25 by the end of next week, the RDIF's Dmitriev said. However, large shipments of the shot have only been sent so far to Argentina, which has received enough doses to vaccinate about 500,000 people.

The sovereign wealth fund also said vaccinations using Sputnik V will begin in a dozen countries including Bolivia, the United Arab Emirates, Venezuela and Iran.

Dmitriev said production had started in India and South Korea and would launch in China this month. Trial doses have also been produced by a manufacturer in Brazil.

 - **Dubai** will start vaccinating people with the Oxford-AstraZeneca COVID-19 vaccine, the state media office said today as the United Arab Emirates battles its biggest outbreak since the pandemic begun.

The first shipment has arrived from India, the state media office said in a tweet. It did not provide details on how many doses were received or when inoculations would start.

February 3 - **Hungary** - Budapest will receive its first 40,000 doses of Russia's Sputnik V COVID-19 vaccine tomorrow - enough to vaccinate 20,000 people, Hungarian Foreign Minister Peter Szijjarto said.

"The first shipment will arrive today based on the deal we signed in Moscow," Szijjarto said in a video on his Facebook page.

"Under a deal signed last month, Russia will ship 2 million doses of the vaccine to Hungary in the coming three months, enough to inoculate 1 million people," Szijjarto said.

He said, "The National Public Health Centre would put the vaccine shipment through tests before the shots are distributed."

– **USA** - People previously infected with coronavirus may only need one dose of the vaccine, a new study suggests.

Researchers found that participants who had contracted COVID-19 in the past and received one shot had antibody levels similar to - and even higher than - those who had never been infected and were given two doses.

Additionally, virus survivors were more likely to report side effects after being immunized such as pain at the injection site, fever, and fatigue.

The team, from the Icahn School of Medicine at Mount Sinai in New York, says giving previously infected individuals only one dose would spare them from unnecessary pain and free up many urgently needed vaccine doses.

February 4 - **AstraZeneca** and Oxford University have co-developed a 'next generation' COVID-19 vaccine to tackle new coronavirus variants, and it could be available in the autumn, its executive vice-president said yesterday. "We're very much aiming to try and have something ready by the autumn, of this year," Mene Pangalos said.

AstraZeneca has already co-developed a COVID-19 vaccine that is authorised for emergency use in the UK, the EU, and seven other countries, but there is a drive for new vaccines that specifically target the COVID-19 variants. Studies suggest the shots available right now may not work as well on certain variants, especially against a mutation found in the variant from South Africa. This mutation has also been detected in some cases of the variant found in the UK and both of these variants have been identified in the US.

"We're working very hard and we're already talking about not just the variants that we have to make in laboratories, but also the clinical studies that we need to run," Pangalos said.

Pfizer and Moderna drug makers that have also developed existing COVID-19 shots are also working on ways of protecting against coronavirus variants too.

- **UK** - Volunteers are being sought for a world-first trial to establish the efficacy of giving people a first dose of one vaccine and a second dose of a different vaccine. The trial, which is being run by Oxford University and is funded by the government's vaccine taskforce, has been described by ministers as 'hugely important.'

It will recruit 820 people over the age of 50 who have not yet had a vaccine, to receive a first dose of either the Oxford/AstraZeneca vaccine or the Pfizer/BioNTech vaccine. Some people will then get an alternative vaccine at a second appointment within 12 weeks, and others will get the same vaccine again.

Public Health England's Green Book on vaccinations already tells the NHS that in exceptional circumstances if people arrive for their second dose and the vaccine they originally had, is not available, they can be given a different one.

Scientists want to know whether protection from mixing vaccines is the same, reduced or even better, compared with adhering to the same vaccine throughout.

With the steady supply of vaccines always in question, the researchers said the information they collect would be useful not only for the UK but for the whole world.

- India - Biotech company Dimerix (ASX:DXB) is on track in the exciting new study to test the effectiveness of its DMX-200 as a treatment option for COVID-19.

The 2.0 CLARITY (Controlled evaluation of Angiotensin Receptor Blockers for COVID-19 respiraTorY disease) clinical trial is expected to begin dosing patients soon in India, where as many as 13,000 people a day are still being diagnosed with the respiratory ailment.

Lead investigator Professor Meg Jardine, a nephrologist and professor of medicine at the University of Sydney, says the study will begin enrolling the first 600 COVID-19 patients as soon as it receives ethics approval.

The CLARITY 2.0 study complements another already underway, looking at the efficacy of angiotensin receptor blockers (ARBs) to treat COVID-19.

COVID-19, Prof Jardine explains, appears to hijack the body's renin-angiotensin system - tilting it towards inflammation and fibrosis.

ARBs such as Avapro (irbesartan), Cozaar (losartan) and Benicar (olmesartan) have been used for about three decades to treat illnesses such as high blood pressure, heart failure and diabetic kidney disease.

February 4 - **North Korea**, which has yet to record a single case of coronavirus, is expected to receive nearly two million doses of the Oxford/AstraZeneca vaccine. According to the COVAX vaccine-sharing programme, the Asian state has been allocated 1,992,000 doses of the vaccine for the first half of this year. The supply will come from the 240 million doses licensed to the Serum Institute of India, the world's largest vaccine manufacturer.

February 5 - **Iran** has received its first batch of foreign-made coronavirus vaccines, as the Middle East's worst-hit country in terms of deaths seeks to stem the pandemic.

Iran's ambassador to Russia, Kazem Jalali, previously said the first shipment would consist of 10,000 doses. Healthcare workers and medically vulnerable groups will receive the first doses of the shots.

February 9 - In an interview on CNBC today, Johnson & Johnson's CEO, Alex Gorsky discussed how the virus has kept mutating, with variants popping up in the UK, South Africa and Brazil.

Gorsky warned that if the virus keeps mutating, and new variants keep getting discovered, the COVID-19 vaccine may become like a seasonal flu shot that is administered every year.

February 7 – **UK** - Covid restrictions likely to continue 'for some time,' says scientific adviser.

Cases of COVID-19 are still falling across the country, according to the latest Public Health England (PHE) report, with the southwest recording the lowest rate – 120.3 per 100,000 people in the past 7 days.

According to the data, 30 to 39-year-olds are seeing the highest number of cases at 265.3 per 100,000, down week-on-week from 367.2. For people aged 80 and over, the rate fell from 294.6 to 200.5. It comes as a new scientific trial discovered that a drug used to treat rheumatoid arthritis could help prevent one in 25 deaths among patients admitted to hospital with Covid.

February 11 - People who have been fully vaccinated against COVID-19 and don't have any symptoms don't have to quarantine if they're exposed to someone with the disease, the Centers for

Disease Control and Prevention said in new guidelines released today. They should still follow other public health guidelines, like wearing a mask.

February 12 - The Canadian province of **Manitoba** said on Thursday it will buy 2 million doses of a COVID-19 vaccine candidate now in early trials, bypassing the national government.

The province's government has agreed to buy the doses from Alberta-based Providence Therapeutics, Premier Brian Pallister said. The company is developing a candidate similar to those produced by Pfizer Inc and Moderna Inc. The premier of Alberta also said his government is pursuing vaccine supplies because of delays in the federal government procuring doses internationally.

If approved by the regulator, Health Canada, Providence would supply Manitoba with its first 200,000 doses next year. Pallister did not release financial terms. Health Canada officials could not be immediately reached for comment.

In total, Manitoba will buy 2 million doses for the province of 1.4 million people. Emergent BioSolutions would manufacture the doses and fill vials at its plant in Winnipeg.

Pallister, a Progressive Conservative, has been critical of Liberal Prime Minister Justin Trudeau for not delivering vaccines fast enough.

Canada's rate of vaccination lags far behind rates per capita in the United States, the United Kingdom and other countries, but the number of new infections is dropping sharply amid widespread health restrictions.

Alberta Premier Jason Kenney at a news conference that Providence told him the company would need a C$150 million order representing 50 million doses to be able to establish a domestic production facility in Canada.

The Canadian government has signed all procurement deals for vaccines so far - more per capita than any other country - but they are all made outside Canada and only Pfizer and Moderna have regulatory approval.

Last week, Canada signed its first deal to allow a foreign coronavirus vaccine, developed by Novavax Inc, to be manufactured domestically.

- The **West African** state of Ivory Coast on Friday reported that 17 people had died of coronavirus in 10 days, with the trend raising fears of an 'explosion' of the disease.

The country has recorded 30,526 cases of Covid-19, of which 171 have been fatal - 17 from February 1 to 11, the health ministry said.

"The epidemic's rebound is characterised by active circulation (of the virus) in the community, which raises fears of an explosion," Health Minister Eugene Aka Aouele told a press conference.

He said there were 'strong suspicions' that the UK variant of the virus, which is more contagious than the original strain in the Covid pandemic, was spreading.

He called on the public to step up efforts to keep the virus at bay by increasing social distancing measures, carrying out tests at schools, limiting movement and avoiding gatherings.

Unlike other African countries, the Ivory Coast does not have a lockdown or curfew, and mask-wearing is required only in enclosed public spaces. Shops, restaurants, bars and nightclubs are open.

The country says it will start immunisation in mid-February despite a delay in deliveries of Pfizer/BioNTech and Moderna vaccines, which had been scheduled to arrive in late January.

February 13 - Vulnerable housebound people in some areas of the **UK** have still not been vaccinated against Covid - while in other areas much younger, fitter people are already receiving the vaccine.

- **Japan's** first batch of COVID-19 vaccine arrived yesterday, local media reported, with official approval for the Pfizer Inc shots expected soon as the country races to control a third wave of infections ahead of the Olympic Games.

- **New Zealand** Prime Minister Jacinda Ardern said on Friday the country's COVID-19 inoculation program will likely begin on February 20th, brought forward by the earlier receipt of the Pfizer-BioNTech vaccine than originally anticipated.

Pressure has been mounting on Ardern to start vaccinations for the country's 5 million people to take advantage of its rare position of having virtually eliminated the virus domestically.

"Last year we indicated the vaccine would arrive in quarter two, and earlier this year we updated that to quarter one," Ardern told reporters. "It's pleasing to be receiving doses this early in quarter one."

Both New Zealand and neighbouring Australia have formally approved the vaccine jointly developed by U.S. drug maker Pfizer Inc and Germany's BioNTech. Australia has said it expects to begin inoculations by the end of this month, without giving a specific date.

February 14 – **British** government scientists are increasingly finding the coronavirus variant first detected in Britain to be deadlier than the original virus, a devastating trend that highlights the serious risks of this new phase of the pandemic.

The British government did not publicly announce the updated findings, which are based on roughly twice as many studies as their earlier assessment and include more deaths from cases of Covid-19 caused by the new variant, known as B.1.1.7.

 - **Lebanon** gave its first COVID-19 vaccines dose to a doctor and an elderly actor today, as it started an inoculation drive it hopes will keep the pandemic in check amid deepening economic crisis. Healthcare workers and those above 75 years are the first in line to be vaccinated under the national roll-out plan.

February 18 – **UK** - One of the largest and most authoritative coronavirus surveys has found that infections are falling in England, confirming that lockdown is working to suppress the virus. Imperial College London's REACT study found that infections had fallen by more than two-thirds since the last time it reported in mid-January.

Professor Paul Elliott, director of the programme at Imperial, called the results 'encouraging,' saying they showed that 'lockdown measures are effectively bringing infections down.'

He added: "It's reassuring that the reduction in numbers of infections occurred in all ages and in most regions across the country."

– **Canada** - Researchers urge delaying Pfizer vaccine's second dose as the first dose is highly effective. The second dose could be delayed in order to cover all priority groups as the first one is highly protective, two Canada-based researchers said in a letter published in the New England Journal of Medicine.

- **Thailand**'s second domestically developed vaccine will soon undergo human trials, officials say, adding that the plan was to produce up to five million doses by the end of the year. The vaccine, developed by Thailand's Chulalongkorn University, had been successful in trials on mice and monkeys and is due to be tested on humans in late April or early May, Kiat Ruxrungtham of the Chula Vaccine Research Center said today.

February 20 – **Israel** - A single dose of the Pfizer/BioNTech vaccine gives people 85% protection from Covid-19, according to a study from Israel.

Pfizer has consistently said that two doses of the vaccine are needed for high efficacy. In clinical trials, it reported efficacy of 52.4% after one dose, but 95% after two doses.

The UK government in December nonetheless decided on a policy of giving as many people as possible a first vaccine shot by increasing the gap between doses of the Pfizer and the Oxford/AstraZeneca vaccine. The second dose is now given up to 12 weeks after the first.

Kinds of Vaccines being developed at this time:

Since the start of the pandemic, scientists around the world have been racing to develop a vaccine that prevents Covid-19.

In December, the Pfizer/BioNTech coronavirus vaccine beat its rivals to be the first approved for use in the UK. Two more vaccines, from Moderna and Oxford/AstraZeneca, have since been authorised, and there is a fourth, fifth, and sixth potentially on the way.

One is the Janssen vaccine, from American company Johnson & Johnson, the world's first single-shot Covid vaccine, which was found to be 66% effective at preventing moderate to severe Covid-19 but offers high protection against people needing to go to hospital, according to trial results.

Meanwhile, the Government has ordered 60 million doses of another Covid vaccine candidate from Novavax, which is due to be made on Teeside if approved. The vaccine was found to be 80.3% effective at preventing Covid-19 in UK trials and worked against the new Kent and South African variants.

The large-scale manufacturing of another potential vaccine made by the French company Valneva, started in Scotland in January. It is expected to deliver up to 60 million doses to the UK by the end of this year if approved.

Here are the differences between the vaccines:

Pfizer/BioNtech: Trials have shown the Pfizer/BioNtech vaccine to be more than 90% effective, but it has to be stored at minus 70 degrees C so is not the easiest vaccine to use. Patients need two doses.

It is known as a messenger RNA (mRNA) vaccine. Conventional vaccines are produced using weakened forms of the virus, but mRNAs use only the virus's genetic code.

An mRNA vaccine is injected into the body where it enters cells and tells them to create antigens. These antigens are recognised by the immune system and prepare it to fight coronavirus. No actual virus is needed to create an mRNA vaccine. This means the rate at which it can be produced is dramatically accelerated. As a result, mRNA vaccines have been hailed as potentially offering a rapid solution to new outbreaks of infectious diseases.

In theory, they can also be modified reasonably quickly if, for example, a virus develops mutations and begins to change. mRNA vaccines are also cheaper to produce than traditional vaccines, although both will play an important role in tackling Covid-19. One downside to mRNA vaccines is that they need to be stored at ultra-cold temperatures and cannot be transported easily.

Sanofi's mRNA COVID-19 vaccine candidate developed by Sanofi and U.S. group Translate Bio 'will not be ready this year,' the French drug maker's chief executive told Le Journal du Dimanche newspaper.

Moderna: This vaccine works in a similar way to the vaccine from Pfizer/BioNTech.

Coronavirus is studded with 'spike proteins' that it uses to enter human cells. Covid-19 vaccines target this spike protein. The Moderna and Pfizer vaccines use synthetic messenger RNA (mRNA), a genetic material that contains information about the spike protein. The vaccines provide the body with instructions to produce a small amount of this protein which, once detected by the immune system, leads to a protective antibody response.

Moderna's vaccine does not require the same ultracold storage as Pfizer's and can remain stable at normal fridge temperature for 30 days. Trials on more than 30,000 people in the US have shown the Moderna vaccine to be 94% effective in preventing coronavirus and Moderna has not identified any significant safety concerns and its vaccine has been approved for use in the US.

The MHRA accepted the recommendation of the Commission on Human Medicines and authorised the Moderna Vaccine on January 8, 2021.

Oxford/AstraZeneca

The vaccine developed by the University of Oxford and pharmaceutical giant AstraZeneca was approved by the MHRA in December last year. The Oxford vaccine is not an mRNA vaccine. Instead, it uses a harmless weakened version of a virus that causes the common cold in chimpanzees.

Oxford data indicates the vaccine has 62% efficacy when one full dose is given followed by another full dose, but when people were given a half dose followed by a full dose at least a month later, its efficacy rose to 90%. The combined analysis from both dosing regimes resulted in an average efficacy of 70.4 %. In separate research, results showed the vaccine offers 76% protection up to three months after the first dose and could reduce transmission by 67%.

However, a study of around 2,000 people has shown the vaccine only offers minimal protection against mild disease of the South Africa variant and, due to the young age of participants, could not conclude whether the vaccine worked against severe disease.

Health minister Edward Argar said on Monday that Oxford researchers remained confident their vaccine could prevent severe disease for those affected by the variant and that booster vaccines to tackle new strains are already in the pipeline.

Valneva: Clinical trials are still ongoing for this vaccine, but manufacturing has started at the French biotech company's site in Livingston, West Lothian.

The candidate is currently in phase one/two trials and will need approval from the Medicines and Healthcare products Regulatory Agency (MHRA) before it is rolled out. Initial results from the ongoing clinical study, involving 150 participants at testing sites in Bristol, Southampton, Birmingham and Newcastle, are expected in April.

The vaccine works by using technology already used in existing vaccines that are used for prevention of diseases such as the flu and Japanese encephalitis. It uses inactivated whole particles of SARS-CoV-2 to induce a strong immune response.

Novavax: This fourth Covid-19 vaccine could be approved for use in the UK within weeks, as late-stage trials suggested it was 89% effective in preventing coronavirus. The vaccine is the first to show in trials that it is effective against the new virus variant found in the UK.

The UK has secured 60 million doses of the vaccine – to be produced on Teesside – which is believed to offer protection against the new UK and South African variants.

It was shown to be 89.3% effective at preventing coronavirus in participants in its Phase 3 clinical trial in the UK, which involved more than 15,000 people aged between 18-84, of which 27% were older than 65, Novavax said.

The vaccine will now be assessed by the Medicines and Healthcare products Regulatory Agency (MHRA), Prime Minister Boris Johnson said.

Pfizer and Moderna vaccines rely on technology that has not been used in previous vaccines, but the Novavax vaccine uses a more traditional method of recreating part of the spike protein of the virus to stimulate the immune system.

Like the Oxford vaccine, the Novavax vaccine can be stored at regular fridge temperature - which means it can be distributed more easily.

In the South African part of the trial, where most of the cases were the South African variant of the virus, the vaccine was 60% effective among those without HIV.

Johnson & Johnson: The Janssen vaccine, from American company Johnson & Johnson could become the sixth vaccine to be approved in the UK. The firm said the vaccine was 85% effective in preventing severe disease 'and demonstrated complete protection against Covid-19-related hospitalisation and death as of day 28.'

The vaccine worked across multiple variants of coronavirus, including the South African variant which has been worrying scientists, the firm said. The UK has secured access to 30 million doses of the Janssen vaccine from Johnson & Johnson.

The vaccine is estimated to remain stable for two years at minus 20C and at least three months at 2-8C, which will make the logistics of rolling the vaccine out easier as it can be stored in a standard fridge. It could be available at designated vaccination sites across the UK, alongside existing vaccines.

British regulators have been conducting a so-called rolling review of the data from Johnson & Johnson. This means that rather than waiting until the end of the clinical trial to assess the data, experts from the MHRA have been assessing data on a rolling basis during the trial and helped speed up the approval process.

February 12 - Covid-19 vaccines are set to be tested on children and potentially even newborns. AstraZeneca, which produces the Oxford vaccine, says it is expanding trials to children as young as six, and The Mail on Sunday can reveal that fellow vaccine maker Janssen, part of Johnson and Johnson, is now looking into testing on newborn babies and even pregnant women.

Vaccine Tests to date:

1. Ellume – Rapid at-home nasal swab test bought over the counter.

2. Azova saliva serum antibody tests that cost $130.00 that can be ordered online.

Covid-19 vaccine rollouts as of February 22, 2021:

Italy: About 5% of the nation has received at least one dose of the Oxford vaccine. Rome's airport has become a vaccine hub, capable of delivering 3,000 vaccines a day.

US: More than 17% have received at least one dose with 1.64 million people per day being vaccinated.

UK: More than 23% have received the vaccine. They bought more than 400 million vaccine doses of the Oxford vaccine.

Australia: Vaccines will start on February 22 to priority groups. The plan to vaccinate all Australians will take up till October 2021. First jabs will be with 80,000 Pfizer doses then more than a million jabs a week using the AstraZeneca one. First in line are aged care residents.

India: Less than 1% of the population have been protected. It hopes to have 250 million people vaccinated by July 2022.

Russia: About 3% have received at least one dose using the Sputnik V vaccine. 58% of the population don't want to take the vaccine.

Germany: Has launched a new plant to make the Pfizer and Oxford vaccines hoping to give tens of millions of doses per month by the end of the year.

UAE: Almost half the population has received at least one dose using the Chinese SinoPharm vaccine and will build a plant there to increase manufacturing.

Bahrain: Over 16% have received at least one dose and will use Pfizer, BioNTech, SinoPharm and Oxford vaccines.

China: About 3% have received at least one dose of the Chinese-made vaccine. The Chinese communist Party will use its vaccine to buy leverage with other smaller nations in the region making it a significant security threat for Australia.

Israel: Almost 75% of the population have received at least one dose using the Pfizer vaccine.

France: About 4.5% have received at least one dose of the Oxford vaccine.

Mexico: .5% have received at least one dose of Sputnik V vaccine.

February 24 - The **United States** and **United Kingdom** are on course to achieve herd immunity against COVID-19 by the end of 2021 given the speed of their mass vaccination programmes, but key European Union nations are not, according to a new report.

The German database firm Statista studied the number of COVID-19 vaccines that were given on a daily basis, using recent data from local health authorities of each country.

In a study published yesterday citing figures from February, it said while the US and UK administered 1.6 million and 434,444 doses on average per day, Germany gave 110,714, France gave 96,706, and Italy gave 67,887.

"Only the UK and US are administering sufficient daily COVID-19 vaccines to achieve herd immunity by the end of 2021. In contrast, EU countries would have to nearly triple the current number of daily vaccine administrations to reach the target," Statista said.

The US and UK 'are already on a promising path,' Statista said, despite having been badly hit by the pandemic – registering the world's worst and fifth-worst death tolls respectively.

The report predicted the US is on course to become the first G20 country to reach herd immunity, and that the UK will become the first large European nation to do so.

In the UK, more than a third of the adult population have so far received a first dose of a vaccine since early December – a widely praised feat the report cited as a reason for the country's progress.

It is not yet known what proportion of a population must be vaccinated against SARS-CoV2 – the virus that causes COVID-19 – to achieve herd immunity, according to the World Health Organization (WHO).

– **US** - FDA releases new data on Johnson &Johnson's single-dose coronavirus vaccine showing it's safe and effective. J&J's single-dose coronavirus vaccine just got one step closer to reaching the public, as US regulators released documents showing the vaccine was safe and confirming that it can help prevent COVID-19.

The Food and Drug Administration's 62-page review of the data found it to be effective and safe, and regulators said there were no identified safety issues that would prevent an emergency okay. The vaccine is widely expected to become the third COVID-19 vaccine to reach the American public.

The healthcare giant has said it will have nearly four million doses ready to ship upon emergency authorization and is on track to deliver 100 million doses to the US by the end of June.

Like the two other US-authorized vaccines, those doses will be available at no cost to individuals in the US. The US government agreed in August to pay $US1 ($1) billion to J&J for 100 million doses and the healthcare giant has pledged not to sell doses for a profit during the pandemic.

Tomorrow, the FDA will convene a panel of independent experts to debate and ultimately vote on whether or not to recommend J&J's jab for a regulatory OK. Experts widely expect the committee to vote in favour, and for the FDA to greenlight the vaccine soon after.

February 25 – **UK** - The team behind the Oxford coronavirus vaccine is assessing the possibility of creating tablets or nasal sprays to replace injections in the future, lead researcher Sarah Gilbert has said.

Appearing in front of the Commons Science and Technology Committee, Professor Gilbert also warned that easing Covid restrictions too quickly could result in higher transmission and increase the risk of new variants emerging with more resistance to existing vaccines.

February 27 - People who had COVID-19 develop strong immunity after a single vaccine dose - so they might need only one shot. An emerging body of research suggests that people who already got a coronavirus infection mount a stronger immune response to their first shot than those who never had the disease.

That could mean that people with a history of infection don't need a second shot to sufficiently protect them from getting sick again.

The following are some of the new mutations:

🇬🇧 **KENT**

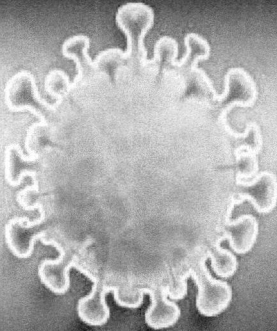

Name: B.1.1.7
In UK? 84,409
Key mutations:
N501Y – speeds up
transmission

🇬🇧 **BRISTOL**

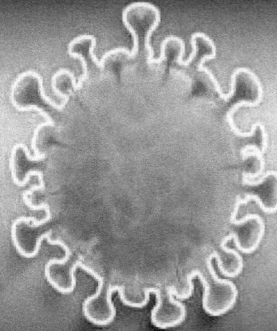

Name: VOC-202102/02
In UK? 30
Key mutations: Kent
variant with E484K, which
can 'escape' antibodies for
other variants

🇿🇦 **SOUTH AFRICA**

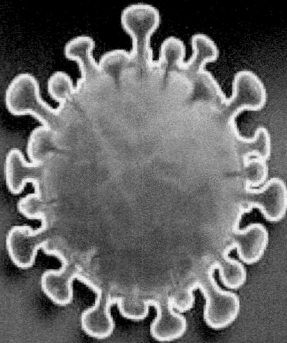

Name: 501Y.V2 or B.1.351
In UK? 258
Key mutations: N501Y
speeds up transmission
E484K can 'escape'
antibodies for other variants

🇧🇷 **BRAZIL #1**

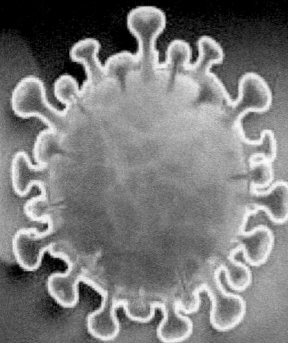

Name: P.1
In UK? 0
Key mutations: N501Y
speeds up transmission
E484K can 'escape'
antibodies for other variants
K417T unknown effects

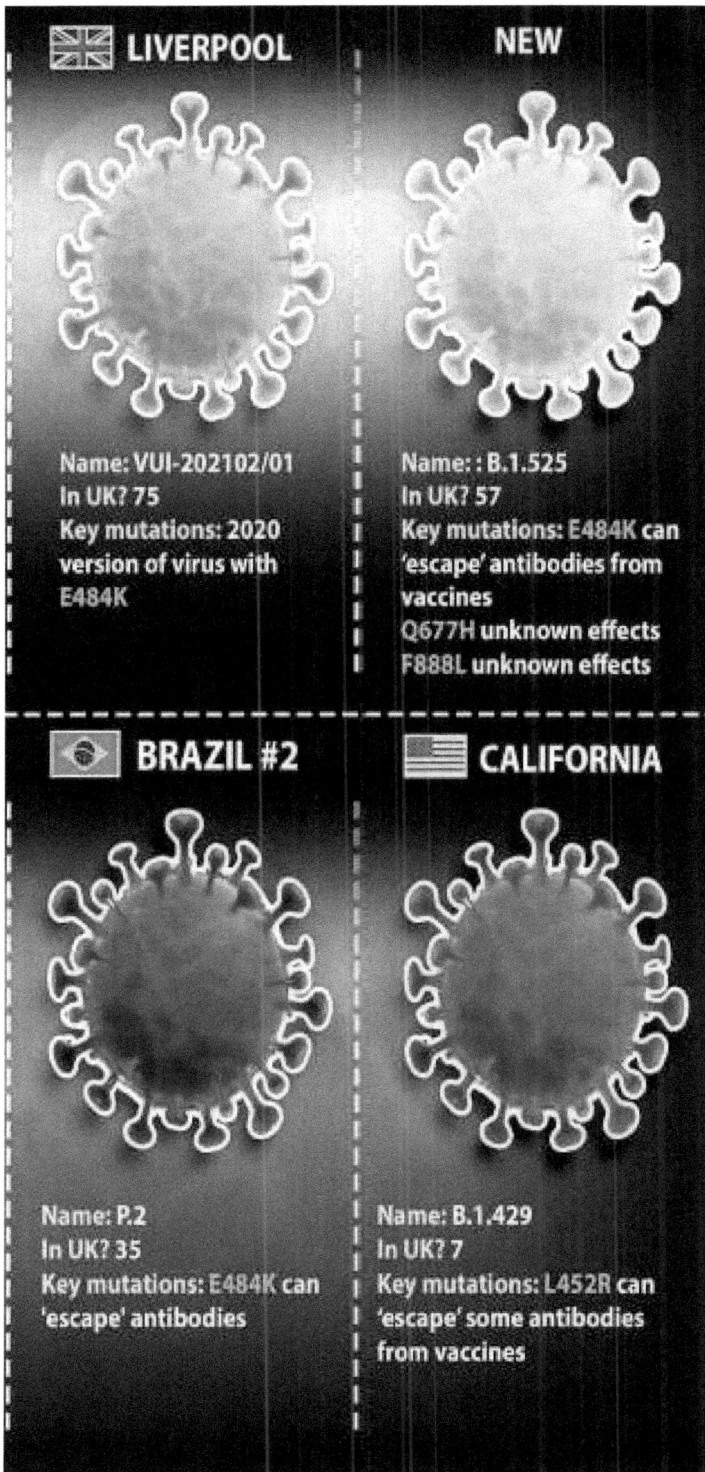

LIVERPOOL

Name: VUI-202102/01
In UK? 75
Key mutations: 2020
version of virus with
E484K

NEW

Name: : B.1.525
In UK? 57
Key mutations: E484K can
'escape' antibodies from
vaccines
Q677H unknown effects
F888L unknown effects

BRAZIL #2

Name: P.2
In UK? 35
Key mutations: E484K can
'escape' antibodies

CALIFORNIA

Name: B.1.429
In UK? 7
Key mutations: L452R can
'escape' some antibodies
from vaccines

CHAPTER 4

USA GOVERNMENT ACTION

August 9 – **President Donald Trump** cut unemployment benefits by $400.00.

The US has surpassed 150,000 deaths from coronavirus, with cases rising in 20 states, as negotiations in Congress over a relief package for Americans broke down again.

August 11 – 54,443 new cases. Deaths – a spike with 10,880 deaths.

There was a shooting near the White House and Donald Trump was evacuated. A 51-year-old man said he had a weapon. He shot his weapon and was shot by SS agents. Eight minutes later, Donald Trump appeared without wearing a mask.

August 15 – 12,890 deaths.

August 19 – New cases 43,798 [Total cases 5,563,646.] Deaths 1,369. Total deaths to date 173,713

- Former US president Bill Clinton eviscerated Donald Trump's coronavirus response in a speech today, saying the President 'ignored' expert advice he didn't like, and told the American people the virus would 'disappear.'

The former first lady Michelle Obama was given the job of closing out day one of the Democratic National convention. She gave exactly the kind of speech that slot demands.

She delivered sweeping statements about what it means to be American then she slammed Donald Trump. "So, let me be as honest and clear as I possibly can. Donald Trump is the wrong president for our country. He has had more than enough time to prove that he can do the job, but he is clearly in over his head. He cannot meet this moment. He simply cannot be who we need him to be for us. It is what it is."

August 20 - It took nearly four years, but former president Barack Obama gave Democrats something they'd been long pleading for - a full-throated attack on Donald Trump.

"I did hope, for the sake of our country, that Donald Trump might show some interest in taking the job seriously; that he might come to feel the weight of the office and discover some reverence for the democracy that had been placed in his care," Obama said.

"But he never did. For close to four years now, he's shown no interest in putting in the work; no interest in finding common ground; no interest in using the awesome power of his office to help anyone but himself and his friends; no interest in treating the presidency as anything but one more reality show that he can use to get the attention he craves."

He continued on to say that Donald Trump, "Hasn't grown into the job, because he can't. And the consequences of that failure are severe. 170,000 Americans dead. Millions of jobs gone while those at the top take in more than ever. Our worst impulses unleashed, our proud reputation around the world badly diminished, and our democratic institutions threatened like never before."

August 30 – Dr. Anthony Fauci said, "Voters were aware of shootings and riots on the streets – this time in Wisconsin." Joe Biden accused Donald Trump of raising tensions over race and justice in the belief that he will benefit from chaos in Democratic cities. Polls show that voters rate COVID-19, the economy and leadership as their top issues in the election. Mr. Trump referred to Mr. Biden more than 40 times during his speech accepting the Republican nomination. He called Mr. Biden as weak and a Trojan horse for the left who would abolish the suburbs.

September 1 - President Donald Trump toured the violence-ravaged Kenosha, Wisconsin Tuesday and called rioters 'domestic terrorists' while praising police, who he argued shouldn't be demonized for 'choking.'

Blake, a black man, was shot seven times in the back by a white cop in front of his three young children a week in late August, leaving the father-of-six paralysed from the waist down. The incident sparked several nights of protests and then violence in the Wisconsin city.

September 4 – New cases 50,183. There have now been well over 6 million cases.

September 5 – 4,486 new cases – deaths 177.

September 10 - **Washington:** The Trump administration has been forced into damage control after the US President admitted deliberately downplaying the seriousness of the coronavirus early in the pandemic in explosive interviews with veteran journalist Bob Woodward.

Trump gave eighteen on-the-record interviews to the famous Watergate journalist for his highly anticipated new book *Rage*, details of which have been leaked to the media ahead of its arrival in American bookshops next week.

In a February interview with Woodward, Trump described the coronavirus as 'deadly stuff' - even as he was publicly predicting it would miraculously disappear and favourably comparing it to the seasonal flu.

"You just breathe the air and that's how it's passed," Trump said in his February interview.

"And so that's a very tricky one. That's a very delicate one. It's also more deadly than even your strenuous flu."

In March, after his rhetoric on the virus had become more serious, Trump told Woodward: "I wanted to always play it down. I still like playing it down, because I don't want to create a panic."

He also tells Woodward that 'plenty of young people' are vulnerable - different from his public message.

Woodward reports Anthony Fauci, the federal government's top infectious disease expert, saying of Trump: "His attention span is like a minus number. His sole purpose is to get re-elected."

James Mattis, Trump's former defence secretary, reportedly described Trump as 'dangerous' and 'unfit,' saying: "There may have to come a time when we take collective action."

He also reportedly said: "The President has no moral compass."

September 13 - President Trump's rally in Henderson, Nevada tonight, will be held inside an Xtreme Manufacturing warehouse despite state restrictions on mass gatherings.

Trump's recent rallies have been held outdoors and in airport hangers. Thousands of supporters attended, but often without social distancing or widespread mask-wearing during the pandemic.

This will be Trump's first indoor rally since his Tulsa, Oklahoma rally held in June, that despite only filling a third of the stadium's capacity due to underwhelming turnout, was traced to an outbreak by local health officials.

The event will likely violate Nevada's restrictions on indoor gatherings of more than 50 people that was put in place by Democratic Governor. Steve Sisolak last May.

Trump has been outspoken in his opposition to Sisolak, claiming at a 'Latinos for Trump roundtable' today that the governor 'totally shut down' the state and that it is one of the most shut down states, and boasting a crowd of 'tens of thousands' at his Saturday rally despite reports of turnout in the low thousands.

October 1 - About 20,000 Amazon workers tested positive for COVID-19, the company announced.

October 2 - President Donald Trump and first lady Melania Trump have tested positive for the coronavirus this morning following the announcement that his top adviser, Hope Hicks, tested positive. The White House physician said the president was expected to continue carrying out his duties 'without disruption' while recovering. A White House official said that on October 2ⁿᵈ that the president was experiencing mild symptoms but was working from the White House residence. The president's physician said in a memo that "Trump and the first lady, who is 50, are both well at this time and plan to remain at home within the White House during their convalescence."

Trump has spent much of the year downplaying the threat of a virus that has killed more than 205,000 Americans. Despite Mr. Trump's repeated claims that the USA had turned the corner on the pandemic – it is again on the rise, with cases up in 31 states and more than 800 deaths on October 2. He and Mrs. Trump quarantined themselves at the White House. Core staff members were tested and a top aide who travelled with him during the week tested positive.

Trump is 74 years old and clinically obese, putting him at higher risk of serious complications from a virus that has infected more than 7 million people nationwide.

Democratic presidential candidate Joe Biden and his wife Jill tested negative, hours later.

That evening President Donald Trump was flown to the Walter Reed Medical Centre when he developed a fever and cough later in the day. Before his flight he was given a dose of an experimental antibody drug that boosts the immune system. He insisted that his symptoms were mild, but that he felt fatigued. REGN-COV2 is potent but very promising according to experts in England. It is set to be rolled out in clinical trials at 30 UK hospitals.

Trump has also been given the drug Remdesivir, an antiviral treatment which has helped some coronavirus patients recover faster.

October 4 – Trump and Biden had their first debate on September 29 and several others were planned but are now on 'hold' until further notice. Because Trump is in quarantine, he can't travel to campaign in person. One of his claims for re-election is that coronavirus dangers have been blown out of proportion.

If Trump becomes incapacitated, 61-year-old Vice President Mike Pence would become Commander in Chief. Both he and his wife tested negative. If the Republican Party decide Mr. Trump is not capable of running for re-election on November 3rd (in just 31 days) he can be replaced on the ticket. This would require a full vote by the Republican National Congress.

25th Amendment - Section 4 (which has never been invoked) outlines the mechanism by which the President can be removed against his will.

It requires the Vice President, in this case Mike Pence, and a majority of Cabinet officers 'or of such other body as Congress may by law provide' to send a 'written declaration that the President is unable to discharge the powers and duties of his office' to the House Speaker – Ms. Pelosi – and the President pro tempore of the Senate, currently Republican Senator Chuck Grassley.

If that happens, 'the Vice President shall immediately assume the powers and duties of the office as Acting President." 'The Democrats' announcement relates to the 'or of such other body as Congress may by law provide' part.

- Joe Biden, the leader of the Democratic Party has been diligent in wearing a mask and encouraged all others to do the same along with proper handwashing and practicing social distancing. He has made Trump's frequent downplaying of the pandemic and mixed messaging on mask-wearing a central campaign theme.

October 5 - Mr. Trump's medical team said he had not run a fever since October 2nd, and that his liver and kidney function remained normal after the second dose in a five-day course of Remdesivir, an intravenous antiviral drug that has been shown to shorten hospital stays.

Dr. Brian Garibaldi said Mr. Trump was also given the steroid dexamethasone in response to 'transient low oxygen levels.'

"He received his first dose of that yesterday and our plan is to continue that for the time being," Dr. Garibaldi said.

Dexamethasone is shown in studies to improve survival for patients hospitalized with critical COVID-19 who need extra oxygen. But it should not be given in mild cases since it can limit the body's own ability to combat the virus, according to guidelines from the Infectious Disease Society of America. The doctors declined to say what they had found in scans of the President's lungs.

"There's some expected findings, but nothing of any major clinical concern," Dr. Conley said.

He declined to outline those 'expected findings.' The virus can cause pneumonia and other damage that may be visible in scans before it is otherwise apparent.

Mr. Trump has also been being given an experimental treatment, Regeneron's REGN-COV2, as well as zinc, Vitamin D, famotidine, melatonin and aspirin.

Dr. Garibaldi, a specialist in pulmonary critical care said, "If he continues to look and feel as well as he does today, our hope is that we can plan for a discharge as early as tomorrow to the White House where he can continue his treatment course."

The President's campaign vowed that Vice-President Mike Pence, who would assume the presidency if Mr. Trump were unable to carry out his duties, would have an 'aggressive' campaign schedule this week, as would Mr. Trump's three oldest children.

Since then, an alarming White House cluster has emerged, with a string of high-profile staffers close to the president also falling ill including Republican senators Mike Lee, Thom Tillis and Ron Johnson, former White House senior adviser Kellyanne Conway and former New Jersey Governor Chris Christie.

October 8 - Democrats will push to form a commission to probe President Donald Trump's health in their latest bid to remove him from office. House Speaker Nancy Pelosi told reporters about her attacks on the Trump administration for allegedly concealing information about the White House outbreak.

"Mr. President, when was the last time you had a negative test before you tested positive?" she said. "Why is the White House not telling the country that important fact about how this spread into – and made a hot spot of the White House."

President Donald Trump had difficulty speaking at one point during his call-in interview on Fox News that night, clearing his throat to the point of a stifled cough before the sound cut out, leading to a pause lasting several seconds.

Elsewhere in the interview, Trump announced his plans to hold a MAGA rally 'probably in Florida' on October 10th (just eight days after he was tested positive with the virus). He also floated having another in Pennsylvania afterwards, though it remains unclear whether he is still contagious with a highly contagious deadly disease.

US President Donald Trump was at it again overnight, making a series of shocking claims just one hour after it was announced the second presidential debate would be virtual.

Instead, the hotly anticipated event would be held virtually 'in order to protect the health and safety of all involved.'

In interviews and on his own social media accounts, Mr. Trump claimed he was in perfect physical shape, he was immune to COVID-19 and that he refused to take part in a 'ridiculous' virtual debate designed to protect others' health.

The Commission on Presidential Debates announced overnight that October 14th's second presidential debate between Donald Trump and White House hopeful Joe Biden would no longer be held in-person as a result of Mr. Trump's coronavirus infection. If the Commission on Presidential Debates gets its way, moderator Steve Scully and the town hall participants will gather at the Adrienne Arsht Centre for the Performing Arts in Miami for the October 15 event, while Mr. Biden and Mr. Trump will be beamed in from different locations.

The announcement was made on Thursday and has been widely reported in the US media.

"The second presidential debate will take the form of a town meeting, in which the candidates would participate in separate remote locations," the commission said.

"I'm not going to waste my time on a virtual debate. That's not what debating is all about," Trump said in an interview with Maria Bartiromo on the Fox Business Network.

During that interview, he also made several bizarre claims about his health after spending three days being treated for COVID-19 at the Walter Reed National Military Medical Centre, claiming he was 'immune.'

"I'm back because I am a perfect physical specimen and I'm extremely young, and so I am lucky that way," he said.

"I don't have heart problems. I don't have diabetes... perhaps a couple of pounds I could lose here or there. And remember this: you catch it, and then you get better, and then you're immune!"

October 10 – During an interview with Rush Limbaugh, Trump suggested for the first time that he had been close to death, had it not been for the drugs he was given. Trump said the experimental Regeneron antibody cocktail that he took was a 'cure.' It's a 'total game changer' and 'better than a vaccine' he said. White House officials refuse to answer basic questions about his health including the date on which the President first contracted the virus and whether he has tested negative.

Today, the President gave a speech for the first time since testing positive. He stood on a balcony and spoke to 2,000 invited supporters on the South Lawn of the White House. There was some mask-wearing at the October 10 event but very little social distancing amongst the attendees. Trump took his off while he made his speech.

Trump was highly criticized after the Rose Garden event announcing the nomination of Judge Amy Coney Barrett to the Supreme Court. There's been speculation that the Barrett announcement was a 'super-spreader' of the disease.

He will hold a Florida rally next week.

Mr. Trump claims he no longer has the virus and is immune from the disease, as he prepares to re-join the campaign trail.

The President tweeted: "A total and complete sign off from White House Doctors yesterday. That means I can't get it (immune) and can't give it. Very nice to know!!!"

The White House has not yet confirmed that Trump has tested negative for the virus.

During an extended media blitz, Trump falsely claimed that there was a cure. There is no cure for the virus, and still no approved vaccine for the virus.

It is estimated 80 per cent of people who require hospitalisation with COVID-19 will experience post-COVID-19 symptoms. (This means that Trump could have ongoing future problems.)

[One man tested positive for COVID-19 in March and ten days later he was in a very bad way and spent weeks in the Royal Brisbane Hospital's COVID-19 unit. Nine months later he has not improved, although his antibodies are still high. He gained 11 kg, has no energy and suffers from brain fog. About one in four people have aftereffects for months. Persistent pain, lasting cognitive difficulties, long-term inflammation in the lungs, cardiovascular and neurological systems, breathlessness, organ damage and coughs are some of the permanent hallmarks of long COVID.]

October 12 - The president was diagnosed with the respiratory illness on October 2nd and returned to the campaign trail 10 days after he was hospitalized for treatment.

October 16 - Trump again tried to defend his coronavirus response, but also admitted that he may not have taken a test for the virus on the day of the first presidential debate.

The second presidential debate was cancelled over Trump's refusal to participate in a virtual showdown with Biden. Instead, the Biden and Trump town halls aired at the same time on ABC and NBC respectively. It's Trumps third rally since his recovery from COVID-19.

The White House coronavirus task force has expressed growing concern as Trump continues to ignore pandemic precautions at his events.

A super-spreader - a term we didn't much use nine months ago - is a person with a contagious disease who gives it to a lot of other people. In the coronavirus pandemic, super-spreaders have played a big role in spreading the virus. Scientists have identified super-spreaders who have infected dozens of people with the virus, while others with the illness haven't infected anyone at all. Super-spreaders may explain why the coronavirus seems to take over so quickly in some places, but not in others.

The predominantly mask-less crowd cheered as the US President put on a 'Make America Great Again' hat, removed his tie and threw it into the audience at his Iowa rally today. Donald Trump's supporters were not deterred by a huge billboard across the road from his rally labelling the gathering a 'super spreader event.'

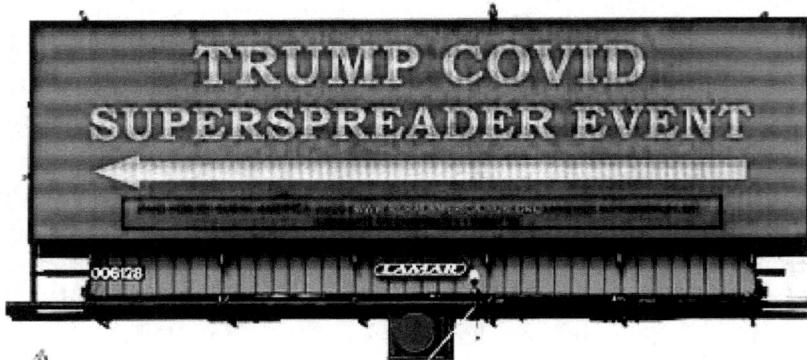

Mr. Trump mentioned that his son Barron had recovered from coronavirus 'within like two seconds' after his wife Melania revealed his diagnosis earlier today. He used this as an argument to get American children back in classrooms.

The president has been subject to widespread criticism for frequently holding crowded, in-person rallies throughout the presidential race. Photographs from Trump's campaign events often show attendees without face masks, against public health guidelines to reduce risks of COVID-19 transmission.

October 17 - For the first time since mid-August, the U.S. has recorded its third consecutive day of more than 50,000 new COVID-19 cases as forecasters predict a death total as high as 233,000 by the end of the month.

At least 57,420 new infections were reported across the country yesterday, bringing the total US infections to over 7.6 million as of today. October 15 and 50,341 reported on October 14. This third 'surge' has resulted in 8,108,811 cases in the US and 221,320 deaths.

Globally there are 39,126,112 cases and 1,101,007 deaths.

- Hours before Donald Trump's arrival in Michigan and Wisconsin, both states reported record-breaking single day coronavirus cases.

Michigan officials reported that on October 15, there were more than 2,000 confirmed cases and on October 16, the state's highest ever single-day coronavirus case count, topping at least 2,015 infections.

In Wisconsin, a record single-day high of 4,041 confirmed cases, according to the state's Department of Health Services. The state saw three consecutive days with at least 3,000 cases.

October 16 - US infections account for the largest single-day spike since July. Nearly 70,000 cases were confirmed this day.

Health officials in the state are urging the president to cancel the campaign event scheduled for 8:00 pm in Muskegon.

Michigan Governor Tony Evers said this week that the president's return is 'encouraging a super spreader event.

"Instead of coming to Muskegon to continue spreading misinformation and packing people close together with Covid-19 cases going up, President Trump should cancel his campaign event and focus on fighting the pandemic with science and evidence," said Dr. Davidson, executive director of the Committee to Protect Medicare.

October 18 - President Donald Trump attended a church service in Las Vegas today. The event, which reportedly took place at the International Church of Las Vegas, drew a large group of congregants to an auditorium-sized indoor space. Those who attended the event were seated side-by-side, and many, including Trump, did not wear face coverings.

Trump's appearance at the Las Vegas church service came shortly after Nevada reported its largest single-day jump in cases of the new coronavirus since August, the Las Vegas Review Journal reported. On October 17, health officials confirmed more than 960 new diagnosis, the most significant daily rise in state-wide infections since mid-August, when close to 1,100 cases were confirmed on a single day.

With nearly 75,000 positive tests and more than 1,400 deaths confirmed, numbers recorded in Clark County alone make up the majority of diagnoses and fatalities confirmed across Nevada. As of October 18, upwards of 90,260 people have tested positive for COVID-19 state-wide, and 1,710 have died as a result. Clark County's per capita infection rate currently exceeds those reported by other hard-hit Nevada counties by at least 1,000 cases per 100,000 people.

October 22 - For almost two months, the White House has been aware of surging cases of COVID-19 across most of the US, but Donald Trump continues to publicly downplay the virus at crowded rallies. Six weekly reports from the White House coronavirus task force, which are not disclosed to the public, but are shared with state governments, were obtained by Democratic representative Jim Clyburn of South Carolina.

Mr. Clyburn, a member of the House Select Subcommittee on the Coronavirus Crisis, released the reports showing that the Trump administration has known since the Labour Day holiday weekend that coronavirus cases were out of control and both mask mandates and increased testing are desperately needed.

"The White House reports released today show that President Trump's contempt for science and refusal to lead during this crisis have allowed the coronavirus to surge," Mr. Clyburn said in a statement. "Contrary to his empty claims that the country is 'rounding the turn,' more states are now in the 'red zone' than ever before. It is long past time that the administration [should] implement a national plan to contain this crisis, which is still killing hundreds of Americans each day and could get even worse in the months ahead."

The reports, published weekly between 16 August and 20 September, underline the disconnect between the task force and the president's public statements and actions. On 1 October, Trump announced that 'the end of the pandemic is in sight.' The next day both he and the first lady tested positive.

October 23 - The United States has hit its highest daily number of Covid-19 cases since the pandemic first began, recording more than 84,218 new cases today. These cases were more than the previous record posted in July of 77,233 new cases in a single day. On October 23rd, the US posted more than 1,100 new deaths, the highest death toll on a single day in more than a month. So, the current impact of the significant rise in cases won't be known for at least three weeks. This comes just a few days after President Donald Trump told the American public that the country was rounding the corner on managing the virus.

Previously, a surge in cases happened in specific areas across the country, such as the coastal states at the start of the pandemic and the Sun Belt during the summertime. But this current surge is considerably more widespread across the country.

Health officials have said the steep incline in cases could be linked to the reopening of schools and increased family gatherings happening across states. With the winter months approaching, people are also spending more time indoors. Coronavirus hospitalisations increased in 38 states last week, and experts have warned an increased death toll could follow in three to four weeks following this surge.

At least 33 states could be designated in the 'red zone' for reporting more than 100 new cases per 100,000 people. There is a lack of beds in several states including Missouri, Idaho and Utah.

In Wisconsin, 90% of hospital ICU beds are full, Governor Tony Evers said. The state opened a makeshift field hospital and accepted its first patient on October 23rd.

This month, hospitalisation rates have doubled in states like Montana, New Mexico, Connecticut and Wyoming.

Dr. Anthony Fauci said that it could be time for a national mask mandate to curb the spread - something Mr. Trump has been against. At the final presidential debate, Trump was asked about the coronavirus cases. His reply was, "We're rounding the turn. We're rounding the corner. It's going away."

Joe Biden claims that there could be a 'dark winter' ahead for the American public because of the rise in new cases.

October 25 - People can now order coronavirus tests from Costco online. The wholesale retailer is selling COVID-19 saliva test kits on its website.

The telemedicine company Azova provides the tests and customers have two options to choose from, the kit with video observation and ones without it.

The kit alone is around $130 dollars. Video observation, which is a virtual session with the company, adds an extra ten dollars to the price tag.

However, before you can receive your test Azova says you must complete a health assessment and register for a lab order.

October 28 - The coronavirus pandemic continued to set records across the US today, even as the administration of President Donald Trump touted its first-term accomplishments in a news release that suggested it had ended the crisis that has cost more than 226,000 American lives and shows no signs of abating.

The US has counted a record 500,000 new infections in the past week, as 20 states, including Illinois, recorded their highest seven-day averages since the start of the outbreak.

The Midwest and Mountain West are in precarious positions with hospitals rapidly filling. Three states, Tennessee, Wisconsin and Oklahoma, suffered record seven-day averages for fatalities, while Oklahoma and Wyoming set records for most deaths in a single day.

The White House in a press release wrote 'Ending the COVID-19 Pandemic' in bold capitalized letters as one of the administration's achievements during Trump's first term.

Dr. Leana Wen, George Washington University School of Public Health said, "There is no sign that points to the US being anywhere close to ending the pandemic; actually, we are trending in all the wrong directions and are in the middle of a coronavirus storm. Downplaying the virus is really dangerous, because letting down our guard enables the virus to spread much more. This is wishful thinking, not the truth."

"There is no metric that points to the US being anywhere close to ending the pandemic; actually, we are trending in all the wrong directions and are in the middle of a coronavirus storm. Downplaying the virus is really dangerous, because letting down our guard enables the virus to spread much more."

Others said members of the White House task force claim the U.S. is still in the throes of a crisis that has killed more Americans than died in combat in World War I and World War II combined.

A new study this week found that a national face-mask mandate could significantly reduce COVID-19 deaths in the next few months, as flu season arrives and as people tend to gather more indoors.

October 30 - The internet is convinced that Donald Trump brought out a fake Melania Trump body double to his latest rally. A video of Melania kissing the President at a rally led to questions from the Internet because not only did Melania look unrecognizable on stage, but in the past, she's never really been affectionate with the President.

November 2 - The U.S. death toll from the coronavirus illness COVID-19 rose above 231,000 today with cases rising in 42 states, as President Donald Trump continued to criticize Dr., Anthony Fauci, a key infectious-disease expert and even hinted he might fire him if he wins tomorrow's presidential election.

Dr. Fauci said, 'The US could not possibly be positioned more poorly. It needs to make an abrupt change in public health practices and behaviours as the holiday season approaches.'

November 3 - US election day. [I couldn't resist adding the following cartoon:]

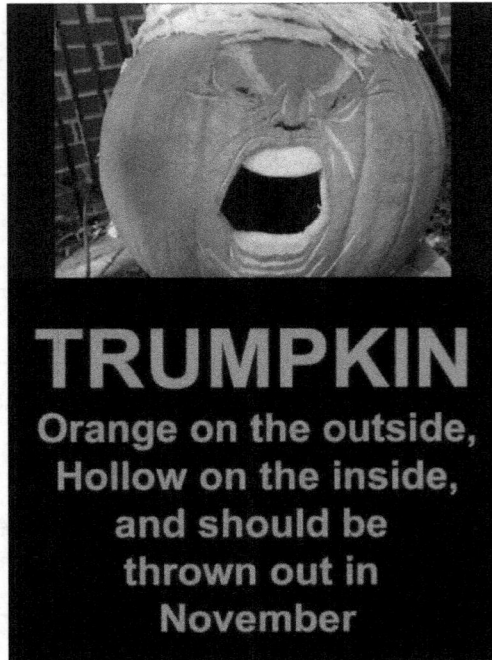

TRUMPKIN
Orange on the outside,
Hollow on the inside,
and should be
thrown out in
November

Government wisdom of the ages

1. In my many years I have come to a conclusion that one useless man is a shame, two is a law firm, and three or more is a congress. - **John Adams.**

2. If you don't read the newspaper you are uninformed, if you do read the newspaper you are misinformed. – **Mark Twain.**

3. Suppose you were an idiot. And suppose you were a member of Congress. But then I repeat myself. – **Mark Twain.**

4. I contend that for a nation to try to tax itself into prosperity is like a man standing in a bucket and trying to lift himself up by the handle. – **Winston Churchill.**

5. A government which robs Peter to pay Paul can always depend on the support of Paul. – **George Bernard Shaw.**

6. A liberal is someone who feels a great debt to his fellow man, which debt he proposes to pay off with your money. – **G. Gordon Liddy.**

7. Democracy must be something more than two wolves and a sheep voting on what to have for dinner. – **James Bovard** Civil Libertarian (1994).

8. Foreign aid might be defined as a transfer of money from poor people in rich countries to rich people in poor countries. - **Douglas Case,** Classmate of Bill Clinton at Georgetown University .

9. Giving money and power to government is like giving whiskey and car keys to teenage boys. - **P. J. O'Rourke**, Civil Libertarian.

10. Government is the great fiction, through which everybody endeavours to live at the expense of everybody else. – **Frederic Bastiat,** French economist (1801-1850).

11. Government's view of the economy could be summed up in a few short phrases: If it moves, tax it. If it keeps moving, regulate it. And if it stops moving, subsidize it. – **Ronald Reagan** (1986).

12. I don't make jokes. I just watch the government and report the facts.- **Will Rogers.**

13. If you think health care is expensive now, wait until you see what it costs when it's free! - **P. J. Rourke.**

14. In general, the art of government consists of taking as much money as possible from one party of the citizens to give to the other. – **Voltaire** (1764).

15. Just because you do not take an interest in politics doesn't mean politics won't take an interest in you! – **Pericles** (430 B.C.).

16. No man's life, liberty, or property is safe while the legislature is in session. - **Mark Twain** (1866).

17. Talk is cheap, except when Congress does it. - **Anonymous**

18. The government is like a baby's alimentary canal, with a happy appetite at one end and no responsibility at the other. - **Ronald Reagan.**

19. The inherent vice of capitalism is the unequal sharing of the blessings. The inherent blessing of socialism is the equal sharing of misery. – **Winston Churchill.**

20. The only difference between a tax man and a taxidermist is that the taxidermist leaves the skin. – **Mark Twain.**

21. The ultimate result of shielding men from the effects of folly is to fill the world with fools. – **Herbert Spencer**, English Philosopher (1820-1903).

22. There is no distinctly Native American criminal class, save Congress. – **Mark Twain.**

23. What this country needs are more unemployed politicians. – **Edward Langley,** Artist (1928-1995).

24. A government big enough to give you everything you want, is strong enough to take everything you have. – **Thomas Jefferson.**

25. We hang the petty thieves and appoint the great ones to public office. – **Aesop.**

Five best ideologies

1. You cannot legislate the poor into prosperity, by legislating the wealthy out of prosperity.

2. What one person receives without working for, another person must work for without receiving.

3. The government cannot give to anybody anything that the government does not first take from somebody else.

4. You cannot multiply wealth by dividing it.

5. When half of the people get the idea that they do not have to work, because the other half is going to take care of them, and when the other half gets the idea that it does no good to work, because somebody else is going to get what they work for, that is the beginning of the end of any nation!

November 4 - The U.S. counted more than 107,872 new cases of the coronavirus illness and at least 1,616 Americans died today, the most in a single day since the start of the outbreak.

This fulfilled a prediction made by Dr. Anthony Fauci in June. Fauci continues to give media interviews and urges Americans to follow safety measures.

The U.S. leads the world by cases with 9.49 million and deaths with 233,777, according to data aggregated by Johns Hopkins University and accounts for more than a fifth of global cases and fatalities.

November 6 – New cases – 121,289.

November 7 – The US election results - As an early lead began to slip on election night, President Donald Trump prematurely declared victory, even as former Vice President Joe Biden appeared set to win thanks to an influx of mail-in ballots, received early but counted last in key states.

Trump has since claimed the race was rigged and shows no sign of conceding, leading the Biden campaign to consider outcomes previously thought to be only the most radical. No network has called the race and the votes are still being counted. Trump has a narrow path to victory in the electoral college. He has never said or implied that he would continue to occupy the White House after exhausting any legal challenges to the vote.

"As we said on July 19th, the American people will decide this election," Biden's team said in a statement November 6th. "And the United States government is perfectly capable of escorting trespassers out of the White House."

"The Secret Service would escort him off, they would treat him like any old man who'd wandered on the property," said one former official involved in the transition process between former President Barack Obama and Trump.

Still, this is what happens when a sitting president doesn't pass the baton to his or her successor. It's never been seen before in the United States and there is no imminent threat that it will happen in January, but there is a plan in place to prevent a transition in power crisis.

The 20th Amendment has it that Trump, or any other lame-duck leader, loses his presidential mandate January 20, 2021 at noon, and, if he tries to stick around after that, the very guard once tasked with protecting the nation's top officeholder now has to evict him. The system is intentionally built to work independently of the whims of whoever happens to be in the White House at the time.

Trump would also lose his commander-in-chief status, meaning the Pentagon cannot and will not come to his aid should Biden be sworn in.

Update - November 7 - People celebrate today in Philadelphia, after Democrat Joe Biden defeated President Donald Trump to become 46th president of the United States.

Republican President Donald Trump's campaign said it had filed suit in Arizona, alleging the Southwestern state's most populous county incorrectly rejected votes cast by some voters in the US presidential race on Election Day.

The lawsuit, filed in Superior Court in Maricopa County, said poll workers told some voters to press a button after a machine had detected an 'overvote.' The campaign contended that decision disregarded voters' choices in those races, saying new voting machines were used on Tuesday November 3rd. The lawsuit suggested those votes could prove 'determinative' in the state's outcome.

November 9 - United States President Donald Trump has tweeted he has 'terminated' Defense Secretary Mark Esper. The move comes days after Mr. Trump's election loss to Joe Biden.

Presidents who win re-election often replace cabinet members, including the Secretary of Defense, but losing presidents have kept their Pentagon chiefs in place until Inauguration Day to preserve stability.

Mr. Trump announced the news in a tweet, saying Christopher Miller, the director of the National Counterterrorism Center, would serve as acting secretary 'effective immediately.'

November 14 - Dr. Mary Trump, Donald Trump's niece and the author of *Too Much and Never Enough: How My Family Created the World's Most Dangerous Man*, said it was 'a given' that the president would never accept the results of any election in which he was not declared the winner.

"He's psychologically incapable of processing this kind of loss," she said, adding that losing an election is 'a unique experience' which her uncle is 'constitutionally incapable of dealing with, processing, or moving on from.'

"Interfering with a peaceful transfer of power is obviously bad, as is undermining the legitimacy of the incoming administration… but who knows what other kind of smash-and-grab activities he's going to engage in? If it was just him doing those things, it would have been starkly obvious that it was just him doing those things, and they would only serve to humiliate him further and delegitimise him," she continued. "But it's not just him, and they are helping him undermine a process that has been in place for over 240 years, and they're doing it in a way that will have lasting damage no matter what happens."

When Biden is sworn into the presidency on Inauguration Day, Trump will become a civilian. If Trump attempted to remain, Biden would have the authority as the new commander in chief to order the military or Secret Service to physically remove Trump from the premises. "The current president's term ends, period," on Inauguration Day, Rick Pildes – professor of constitutional law at the New York University School of Law says. Trump 'would be a trespasser at that point.'

November 15 – When Donald Trump hands over the presidency on January 20th, he will also lose the 'cloak of immunity' which has protected him for four years against a range of lawsuits and prosecutions. Since becoming president, he has been inundated by civil lawsuits and criminal investigations directed at himself, his family and close associates. Mr. Trump's legal team will no longer be able to shield him from having to testify in inquiries levelled against him such as the allegations of Russian interference in the 2016 election and two women who claimed to have had affairs with him before he entered the White House.

The President has the power to pardon, not only people convicted of crimes, but also people yet to face the courts. He has till January 20th to pardon himself. Or he could resign from the White House before the January 20th inauguration of Joe Biden, handing power to his Vice President – Mike Pence who could then pardon his ex-boss.

November 21 - Donald Trump missed a side-event G20 virtual summit centred on pandemic preparedness and was seen playing golf around the time of the event. As the sub-meeting was due to begin today, Mr. Trump had just arrived at his golf course in Virginia and did not appear on the list of speakers for the event.

November 28 – A federal appeals court flatly dismissed President Donald Trump's claim that the election was unfair. It was the latest in more than two dozen court defeats around the country for the Trump campaign.

November 29 – With there being so many anti-vaxxers in the US and that country on the brink of an infection explosion it is obvious to everyone what will happen to the international opening of the country. Hospitals are struggling to cope with nearly 200,000 new infections per day and an average daily death toll of more than 1,500. The virus just keeps steadily steamrolling through the population leaving behind very few with protective antibodies. Anti-vaxxers are a lost cause.

December 10 - US Secretary of State, Mike Pompeo called on US colleges to shut down Chinese 'Confucius Institutes' and limit the number of Chinese students admitted into US colleges, claiming the students were stealing research on behalf of the Chinese government. Confucius Institutes are agreements between foreign and Chinese universities with the purpose of spreading Chinese culture, language and teaching around the world.

The Trump administration has alleged that US colleges are 'massively' underreporting the amount of money they receive from China and other nations the US calls 'adversaries.' Since the schools were targeted by the federal government, they have disclosed an additional $6.5 billion in foreign funding that was previously unreported.

Twelve schools were investigated in the report, including Yale, Harvard, Stanford and Georgetown universities. According to the report, most of the schools had dealings with Huawei, a Chinese technology company that Mr. Pompeo and other US intelligence officials claim is a security threat.

December 11 - Donald Trump is still clinging to the delusion that he could still be President of the United States after 12.01 pm on 20 January 2021 - but most of the thousands of political appointees who serve in his administration have seen the writing on the wall.

The most prominent of those soon-to-be ex-Trump administration officials is his chief law enforcement officer, William Barr. Although the Attorney General has been one of the president's staunchest allies, Barr was recently reported to be considering an early resignation after angering Trump by acknowledging that his evidence-free claims of rampant fraud plaguing the election he lost are just that: evidence-free.

Yet even as Trump continues to claim that he won an election he lost handily and his allies continue filing lawsuits which have rejected by some of the most conservative jurists in the United States, administration officials at all levels have to risk being fired or blacklisted by Trumpworld when they put out feelers for their next career moves. That's because doing so means defying edicts forbidding them to job hunt.

Trump's reluctance to admit he lost the election has created a complicated scenario for those who know they'll be out of work on January 20.

Traditionally, top officials from previous administrations have been sought after by some of the world's largest corporations. But after four years of an administration that seemed to delight in norm-breaking this might not happen.

Whether or not there is any organized effort to pressure employers to 'boycott' ex-Trump staffers, one former senior government official said the administration's brand has become so toxic that many who served will have trouble finding people receptive to hiring them.

December 12 - President Donald Trump and his allies have been on a hot streak trying to overturn the will of more than 81 million voters, losing 29 of the 38 election court cases they have brought so far and winning zero.

Judges aren't having any of it. The judges have struck down the lawsuits for various reasons. Voters - not judges - decide elections they say, and more voters chose President-elect Joe Biden over Trump.

Arizona's Judge Diane Humetewa said, "Plaintiffs also include documents showing that the facts underlying their allegations of ballot counting and verification misconduct occurred weeks before Election Day," she wrote.

Trump and his allies are fighting voting rules that have been on the books for months and sometimes years.

It's been more than a month since voting ended. But almost all the lawsuits from Trump and his allies say election rules in particular states are unconstitutional and that the results should therefore be overturned.

In Wisconsin, the Trump campaign argued that ballots cast by mail because of the coronavirus pandemic (including their top lawyer's ballot) shouldn't have been legal.

In Pennsylvania, the campaign argued that most of the state's votes should be thrown out because some voters were allowed to fix clerical issues on their ballots."

"Prohibiting certification of the election results would not reinstate the Individual Plaintiffs' right to vote. It would simply deny more than 6.8 million people their right to vote," Judge Matthew Brann wrote in a ruling. Brann was dismissing a case the Trump campaign brought in late November to challenge a Pennsylvania voting law passed in October 2019.

In those states as well as Nevada, Arizona, Michigan and Georgia, Republicans sued over what they said was the illegal expansion of mail-in voting in the middle of a pandemic that has killed more than 291,000 people in the US.

December 16 - President Donald Trump is leaving the White House, but he is not going to fade away quietly. He will re-enter private life on January 20th with an array of opportunities. He has told allies he is considering another White House bid.

Trump has already formed a political action committee that will allow him to raise money and exert influence in the party after he leaves office, whether he becomes a candidate or not.

However, he faces a range of civil and criminal legal actions related to his family's businesses and his activities before he took office, which could accelerate once he loses the legal protections granted to the occupant of the Oval Office.

January 5 – Public health experts are warning that the new mutant British variant of the novel coronavirus in the U.S. will make efforts to contain the spread as well as to vaccinate people a 'formidable challenge.' The new strain, known as SARS-CoV-2 VUI 202012/01, is feared to be 70 percent more transmissible and to spread more easily among children.

So far, the 'super-COVID' variant has only been detected in four states: California, Colorado, Florida and New York. But scientists say there are likely 'hundreds' of infections throughout the nation and that there needs to be a stronger push to get people immunized before more people are infected with - or die from - the new strain.

January 6 - Congress met today to certify the Electoral College votes for President-elect Joe Biden. The session was interrupted, however, by violence and the House is now in recess with members of Congress, including Vice President Mike Pence, being led to safety.

A violent mob of pro-Trump supporters overpowered police, broke through security lines and windows and rampaged through the Capitol, forcing politicians to scatter as they were finalising Biden's victory over Trump in the Electoral College. Five people died including a Capitol police officer and a woman was shot in the neck.

Lindsay Watts, a reporter with a Fox News affiliate in Washington, DC, said on Twitter that she'd learned from a paramedic source that one person had been shot and resuscitation efforts were underway. The person who was struck by a bullet was not a uniformed officer. MSNBC reported that a law enforcement officer fired the shot. The circumstances surrounding the shooting remained unclear in the immediate aftermath.

During the riots, multiple injured police officers were seen being evacuated after clashing with protesters.

The US Capitol building is currently under lockdown given the chaos in Washington DC. Mr. Trump had put pressure on Mike Pence to challenge the certification of the Electoral College, but the vice president does not have the power to do so.

Before the riots Trump encouraged thousands of supporters to 'fight like hell'" before they stormed the building.

In a later tweet, Mr. Trump did not tell the rioters to stand down but instead asked that they remain 'peaceful' against Capitol Police and other members of law enforcement. This tweet came more than an hour after rioters breached the US Capitol and first started to display violence against police officers.

The White House has repeatedly refused to say what the outgoing president will do when Mr. Biden is inaugurated on 20 January, prompting speculation about whether Mr. Trump will attend the ceremony.

The US president, who was defeated in November's election, is reportedly considering travelling to his Turnberry golf resort in Scotland to avoid Mr. Biden being sworn into office. Mr. Biden won the presidency with 306 electoral votes to Mr. Trump's 232. He received 81,283,485 votes versus the incumbent's 74,223,744, a margin of more than seven million in the popular vote.

Vice President, Mike Pence will attend the upcoming inauguration of Joe Biden, multiple media reports said on January 9th, with the vice president becoming the latest long-time loyalist to abandon an increasingly isolated President Donald Trump. Relations between Trump and Pence - previously one of the mercurial president's staunchest defenders - have nosedived when the vice president formally announced Biden's victory in the November's election.

Scotland's First Minister Nicola Sturgeon says Donald Trump will not be allowed to visit Scotland to play golf during lockdown. "Coming to play golf is not what I would consider to be an essential purpose."

January 7 – New cases in 24 hours – 250,394 – deaths 3,916.

January 9 – The Republican calls for Donald Trump's removal from office are intensifying, as lawmakers condemn the president for inciting the mob of his supporters who stormed and vandalized the US Capitol. That includes a small group of mostly moderate Republican leaders who have condemned Trump and demanded that he resign or be forced out, either by invoking the 25th amendment or impeachment proceedings.

120 Democrats have already signed a letter to initiate a second round of impeachment proceedings against the president and could vote on articles as early as next week. Trump could very well be

impeached a second time, but two-thirds of the Senate would still be needed to convict him before Trump could be removed from office. With Congress officially on a break and the Republicans still in control of the Senate, there is not enough time to make this happen. Alternately, Trump could choose to resign and hand over to Mr. Pence before January 20th.

House Speaker Nancy Pelosi said she had spoken to the chairman of the Joint Chiefs of Staff about preventing the 'unhinged' president from initiating military actions or a nuclear strike.

Twitter and Facebook have placed a permanent ban on Trumps messages due to the risk of further incitement of violence.

January 11 - US House Speaker Nancy Pelosi says the Democrats will proceed with impeachment against Donald Trump within days unless Vice President Mike Pence invokes the 25th Amendment and ousts him himself.

Politicians are set to introduce the legislation later today with voting by the middle of the week.

House speaker Nancy Pelosi's leadership team will also seek a quick vote on a resolution calling on Vice President Mike Pence and Cabinet officials to invoke the 25th Amendment. President Donald Trump faces a single charge of 'incitement of insurrection'" over the deadly riot at the US Capitol, according to a draft of the articles.

"We will act with urgency, because this President represents an imminent threat," Pelosi said in a letter late on Sunday to colleagues emphasising the need for quick action.

"The horror of the ongoing assault on our democracy perpetrated by this President is intensified and so is the immediate need for action."

During an interview on 60 Minutes aired yesterday, Pelosi invoked the Watergate era when Republicans in the Senate told President Richard Nixon: "It's over."

"That's what has to happen now," she said.

The four-page impeachment bill draws from Trump's own false statements about his election defeat to Democrat Joe Biden.

Also cited is his pressure on state officials in Georgia to 'find' him more votes and his White House rally ahead of the Capitol siege, in which he encouraged thousands of supporters to 'fight like hell' before they stormed the building last January 6.

The legislation said: "President Trump gravely endangered the security of the United States and its institutions of Government. He will remain a threat to national security, democracy, and the Constitution if allowed to remain in office," they wrote.

Trump - holed up at the White House - was increasingly isolated. Judges across the country, including some nominated by him, repeatedly dismissed cases challenging the result. Attorney General William Barr, a Trump ally, said there was no sign of any widespread fraud.

Pence has given no indication he would act on the 25th Amendment. If he does not, the House would move towards impeachment.

On impeachment, House Democrats would likely delay for 100 days sending articles of impeachment to the Senate for trial, to allow Biden to focus on other priorities.

Meanwhile, the New York State Bar Association is launching an inquiry into President Trump's personal attorney Rudy Giuliani.

The inquiry will determine whether Giuliani should be removed from the membership rolls of the country's largest voluntary state bar association.

January 14 – Donald Trump has become the first USA president to be impeached twice after the House of Representatives voted to send him for trial in the Senate on charges of inciting insurrection in last week's Capitol riot. The House speaker, Nancy Pelosi, said Trump was a 'clear and present danger to the nation we all love' as she presided over a 232 to 197 vote that included ten Republicans in the 'yes' group.

Mitch McConnell, the outgoing Senate majority leader, said there was 'simply no chance' of concluding a trial in the upper house before Trump leaves office next week. The trial will therefore begin once Joe Biden is inaugurated on January 20th which will require a two-thirds majority in the Senate to convict Trump.

A day after Trump was impeached in Congress for allegedly supporting that attack, more barriers were being erected and razor wire laid was part of precautions ahead of the inauguration. The centre of Washington was on lockdown today as more than 20,000 armed National Guard troops were mobilized due to security concerns ahead of the presidential inauguration of Joe Biden.

Washington Police Chief Robert Contee said the US capital was facing 'a major security threat,' one week after supporters of outgoing President Donald Trump stormed the US Capitol to try to block Biden's confirmation as election winner.

Security officials are warning that extremist Trump supporters, armed and possibly with explosives, pose a dangerous threat to Washington as well as state capitals over the coming week. Most of downtown Washington was off limits to traffic and the Secret Service, in charge of security, was considering an unprecedented shutdown of the entire National Mall - the grassy area normally where hundreds of thousands gather to celebrate the inauguration of a new president.

In steps not seen since after the September 11, 2001 national alerts, an internal FBI bulletin warned that an armed group planned to 'storm' government offices in all 50 states to protest Biden, ABC News reported.

"The FBI received information about an identified armed group intending to travel to Washington, DC on 16 January," the bulletin added.

Political figures boosted their own personal security. Washington Mayor Muriel Bowser has received death threats. Peter Meijer, one of 10 House Republicans who voted with Democrats on Wednesday to impeach Trump for supporting 'insurrection,' said he and other lawmakers were taking precautions like acquiring body armour.

"I have colleagues who are now traveling with armed escorts out of the fear for their safety," he told MSNBC. "Our expectation is that someone may try to kill us."

- Some of the pro-Trump mob that stormed the US Capitol last week aimed to 'capture and assassinate elected officials,' prosecutors have said. Federal prosecutors filed a motion late today in the case against Jacob Chansley, the Arizona man who took part in the insurrection while sporting face paint, no shirt and a furry hat with horns.

Prosecutors said that after climbing up to the dais where Vice President Mike Pence had been presiding moments earlier, Mr. Chansley wrote a threatening note to Mr. Pence that said: "It's only a matter of time, justice is coming."

Prosecutors said that while Mr. Chansley said the note was not meant as a threat, 'the government strongly disagrees.'

Mr. Chansley told investigators he came to the Capitol 'at the request of the president that all `patriots' come to D.C. on January 6, 2021.' An indictment unsealed on January 12 in Washington charges him with civil disorder, obstruction of an official proceeding, disorderly conduct in a restricted building, and demonstrating in a Capitol building.

January 15 - Although President Donald Trump is serving the final days of his presidency, he is expected to continue receiving intelligence briefings even after he leaves the White House. Former FBI Director James Comey, however, is warning future officials about what information they choose to share with Trump.

"That is all controlled by the director of national intelligence, who will have to take a very hard look at whether Donald Trump should be given information, including any information that might be sensitive to the security of the United States for the reasons you said," Comey said.

"The guy's a lying demagogue who you can't trust... be very, very careful about what you give him."

- Several prominent business leaders, including Apple CEO Tim Cook, and Google CEO Sundar Pichai have spoken out against the riot calling on the president to put an end to the chaos. Deutsche Bank, Aon, Cushman & Wakefield, and even New York City are among the entities that have moved to cut ties with Trump's business.

- Joe Biden will take the oath of office and become President of the United States on Wednesday January 20, 2021.

Usually the National Mall, which leads from the Lincoln Memorial, past the Washington Monument to the steps of the Capitol Building

- is packed with people on Inauguration Day. But this year the city has announced the Mall will be entirely closed to the public - an unprecedented shutdown of America's most prominent public monuments - over fears of violent protests.

DC Mayor Muriel Bowser has urged Americans not to come to the city to watch the inauguration, and instead to watch it at home.

January 19 - President Trump is not expected to issue pardons for himself or his family, according to Fox News White House correspondent John Roberts.

White House aides and lawyers have reportedly urged the president not to try to pardon himself or to issue pre-emptive pardons for members of his family, fearing that it might lead to more Republican Senators to vote to convict Mr. Trump in the upcoming Senate impeachment trial. No president has tried to pardon themselves while in office.

Trump has already issued a pardon for one member of his extended family, Charles Kushner, the father of Jared Kushner, but reporting suggests that he will not issue pre-emptive pardons for himself or his kids, despite the danger that some of them, including Mr. Trump himself, may be in legal jeopardy after he leaves office.

The Independent reported that Mr. Trump is planning to dole out up to one hundred pardons and commutations of sentences, which could include some white-collar criminals, in the hours he has remaining in the White House.

Mr. Trump faces two New York state inquiries into whether he misled tax authorities, banks or business partners. Two women alleging he sexually assaulted them are suing him. Some Democrats are calling for the revival of a federal campaign finance investigation that appeared to end under former Attorney General Bill Barr.

Mr. Trump has said that he has the 'absolute right' to pardon himself for any federal offences, but the concept remains untested because no president has ever attempted to do so. A 1974 Justice Department opinion said presidents could not pardon themselves because that would violate the 'fundamental rule that no one may be a judge in his own case.'

Trump has used his pardon power to help friends and high-profile defendants in the past, commuting the sentence of long-time friend Roger Stone in July and former Illinois Gov. Rod Blagojevich in February.

January 20 – **Joe Biden** has been sworn in as the 46th President of the United States, vowing to end the 'uncivil war' in a deeply divided country reeling from a battered economy and a raging coronavirus pandemic. Mr. Biden, led by Chief Justice John Roberts, gave the oath of office on a 127-year-old family Bible just before midday today (local time) at Washington DC's Capitol building.

Mr. Biden was inaugurated as the 46th president at a ceremony at the US capitol, following which the couple was given a military escort to their new home.

The Bidens were momentarily left to wait outside the White House in an awkward moment on Inauguration Day, possibly as a result of a final 'petty' act by the Trump administration.

As the Bidens walked up the steps to enter the executive mansion, pausing to wave before turning to enter, the anticipated moment fell flat as the doors failed to open and the couple was left on the doorstep.

According to the National Journal, a well-placed official not associated with the incoming Biden team told the newspaper: "The Trumps sent the butlers home when they left so there would be no one to help the Bidens when they arrived."

Notably, the chief usher Timothy Harleth who had been scheduled to welcome the Bidens to the White House in the absence of Mr. Trump, had been also abruptly fired five hours earlier.

The chief usher is responsible for the management of the building and oversees residence staff including construction, maintenance, remodelling, food, as well as the administrative, fiscal, and personnel functions.

At 78, Joe Biden is the oldest person to become US president. A short time earlier Kamala Harris became the first black, South-Asian and female American to be vice-president.

Ms. Harris was sworn in by Supreme Court Justice Sonia Sotomayor, the first Latina justice.

In attendance at the ceremony were former US presidents George W. Bush, Barack Obama and Bill Clinton, along with outgoing vice-president Mike Pence. Outgoing president Donald Trump did not attend the ceremony, breaking with more than 150 years of tradition. He left the White House to attend a farewell event at Joint Base Andrews in suburban Maryland before flying to Florida.

As Mr. Trump left the White House, his helicopter flew over thousands of American and state flags planted in the National Mall, standing in for the hundreds of thousands of people who gathered for past inaugurations to watch the proceedings on big-screen televisions. Streets that would typically be lined with thousands of inaugural onlookers were ringed instead with a massive security presence, including military vehicles and armed troops. About 25,000 National Guard members were dispatched to Washington following the violent melee at the US Capitol two weeks ago.

Donald Trump's decision to shun Joe Biden's inauguration has caused serious logistical problems for perhaps the most sensitive section of the presidential handover: the nuclear codes.

During a normal inauguration ceremony, the nuclear football, which contains the equipment the president uses to authenticate his orders and launch a nuclear strike, is handed over from one presidential aide to another at the stroke of noon.

Trump left Washington DC at around 8:00 am, however, and flew to his Florida estate, Mar-a-Lago. As president, he took the nuclear football with him. At all times, the president carries with him a plastic card, known as 'the biscuit,' which contains codes that identify the president, who is the only person authorized to launch nuclear weapons. The Constitution gives Trump control of nuclear attacks until the very second that Biden is sworn in. Trump's 'biscuit' was deactivated at noon, and Biden's came into force. The aide with the 45-pound briefcase containing the nuclear football left Florida and flew back to Washington DC.

As Joe Biden uttered the words "So help me God," his hand on a thick Bible, a wave of blessed relief rippled through millions of Americans – and all those, anywhere, who had lived through the stress of the Trump era. The TV networks had helpfully shown footage of the military aide who carries the nuclear 'football,' the case containing the codes required to launch the mighty US atomic arsenal, and there was comfort in knowing that that aide now answered to Biden, not the man who a few hours earlier had fled to his resort in Florida.

Given his boss's refusal to attend the inauguration, Pence's appearance – and those of other Republicans – looked like an act of defiance, signalling acceptance of the democratic legitimacy of the proceedings. The presence of former presidents – Bill Clinton, George W Bush, Barack Obama – suggested the chain of American democracy remained intact, even if its most recent link was missing and broken.

Americans are officially under management after Joe Biden and his wife Jill arrived at the White House and the new president prepares to sign a suite of executive orders undoing key policies of the Trump administration.

President Biden has vowed to repeal the controversial 'Muslim ban,' re-join the World Health Organization and the Paris Climate Accord.

He will also issue a mask mandate on federal property and interstate travel and work with Congress to pass his proposed $1.9 trillion COVID-19 relief legislative package.

The 78-year-old said he plans to repeal the transgender military ban enacted by President Donald Trump and send an immigration bill to Congress, which seeks to give 11 million undocumented immigrants 'roadmap' to US citizenship.

 - **California** has become the first state to record more than 3 million coronavirus infections, as it grapples with an unprecedented surge of cases that has left hospitals overwhelmed.

That remarkable figure, which comes from Johns Hopkins University, was not entirely unexpected for the nation's most populous state – but the speed at which it arrived has been stunning.

January 23 – Dr. Anthony Fauci admitted he was 'knocked out' for a full day by his second dose of COVID-19 vaccine.

'I was hoping that I wouldn't get too knocked out. I did for about 24 hours. Now I'm fine,' Dr. Fauci said during a January 28 White House press briefing when asked if he'd had his booster shot.

The nation's top infectious disease doctor said he was 'fatigued. A little achy. You know. Chilly,' but 'not sick' after his second dose of Moderna's coronavirus vaccine. Those are among the most common side effects of either of the two shots authorized in the US, made by Pfizer and Moderna. Dr. Fauci revealed he got his second dose of the vaccine on January 19 that came 28 days after he received his first dose of the shot on December 22, on live television.

He joined the ranks of other officials and high-profile figures whose vaccinations were televised to encourage Americans to get theirs, including President Biden, former Vice President Pence and three former US presidents: Obama, Bush and Clinton.

But Dr. Fauci continued to remind Americans that those side effects are not illness triggered by the vaccine, but the immune system ramping up to fend off the virus.

Surveys showed that Americans' top concerns were that, despite published data from large trials, vaccines were developed too fast and might be unsafe or cause side effects some believed were worse than COVID-19 itself.

Since the rollout began, at least 20 cases of severe allergic reactions to Pfizer's vaccine have been documented. No deaths have been conclusively linked to either Pfizer's or Moderna's vaccine. About 55 percent of people who got Moderna's shot in its trial reported side effects after the first dose. Eighty percent of participants who got the real vaccine had side effects after the second dose, so doctors warned Americans to be prepared to feel these. Like Dr Fauci, about 70 percent of participants were fatigued after their second dose and more than half were achy or had chills. Headaches were also a common side effect.

Dozens of Americans who said they took part in trials for Moderna's and Pfizer's vaccines said the second dose had left them with significant side effects, with some reporting being in bed for a day or more or developed high fevers.

- The Centres for Disease Control and Prevention (CDC) has quietly updated its guidance on how late the second dose of a coronavirus vaccine can be administered after insisting it would not allow delays in shots.

Currently, the two vaccines approved by the US Food and Drug Administration (FDA), one by Pfizer-BioNTech and the other by Moderna, are given three weeks and four weeks apart, respectively. But in a new advisory posted to its website on January 28, the CDC said the shots can be given up to six weeks apart.

"The second dose should be administered as close to the recommended interval as possible," the CDC wrote. "However, if it is not feasible to adhere to the recommended interval, the second dose may be scheduled for administration up to 6 weeks (42 days) after the first dose."

It comes as several states report a shortage of shots, leading to concerns the federal government is attempting to stretch the national vaccine supply. So far, a total of 39.8 million doses have been distributed across the country but just 19.1 million have been administered.

January 24 – Joe Biden raced through 27 executive orders on his first three days, reversing Donald Trump's approaches to the pandemic, the economy and international engagement but they are in danger of becoming bogged down because of Donald Trump's impeachment trial.

Democratic Senate leader, Chuck Schumer, confirmed that he will receive the article of impeachment on January 25 and begin the former president's trial next week.

- The fate of Donald Trump's border wall with Mexico will be decided in coming weeks after the new president fulfilled his promise to halt construction. Rather than Mexico paying as Donald Trump promised, American taxpayers have funded the project. The steel wall measures 6 metres to 8.2 metres high.

January 25 – Democrats will send the single article of impeachment to the Senate for a reading tonight. It alleges incitement of insurrection, regarding the 6 January riot at the US Capitol that left five dead, including a police officer.

Republican divisions over Donald Trump's second impeachment trial came into clearer focus yesterday, as the former president spent his first weekend out of office plotting revenge against those, he says betrayed him.

Four days after leaving the White House and stewing over election defeat by Joe Biden, Trump continued to drop hints of creating a new party - a threat some see as a gambit to keep wavering senators in line ahead of the opening of his trial, in the week after 8 February. Trump has said the threat of starting a Maga (Make America Great Again) or Patriot party, gives him leverage to prevent senators voting to convict, which could lead to him being prevented from seeking office again.

"He fired up a crowd, encouraging them to march on the Capitol at the time that the Congress was carrying out its constitutional responsibility to certify the election," Mitt Romney the Utah senator told CNN's State of the Union. "These allegations are very serious. They haven't been defended yet by the president. He deserves a chance to have that heard but it's important for us to go through the normal justice process and for there to be resolution."

Romney said it was constitutional to hold a trial for a president who has left office.

"I believe that what is being alleged and what we saw, which is incitement to insurrection, is an impeachable offence. If not, what is?"

January 26 - The chance of Donald Trump being convicted in his impeachment trial in the Senate looks less likely as of today when 45 Republicans attempted to dismiss the proceedings before they began. With 55 senators still supporting the trial, the Republicans' objections were not enough to derail it, but to get a conviction 67 senators need to vote in favour. In practice, this means a dozen Republicans who just voted to end the trial would need to cross the aisle and vote in favour of impeaching Trump, which seems unlikely.

[**Author's Note:** I'm beginning to understand how cults are formed. Donald Trump had four years to brainwash his followers to believe that what he was doing was for their benefit and what he was saying was the truth - when in fact everything he did was for his own benefit and thus by March 1, 2021 US had a staggering 28,833,03 COVID-19 cases and 517,20 deaths.

Just before he was going to be charged with impeachment, House Speaker Nancy Pelosi said she had spoken to the chairman of the Joint Chiefs of Staff about preventing the 'unhinged' president from initiating military actions or a nuclear strike.

[Not only should Trump be convicted of *impeachment* – he should also be charged with *treason* because he incited radical American terrorists to overthrow the legally elected government.

The definition of Treason in the United States is:

Treason: the crime of betraying one's country. Constitutionally, citizens of the United States owe allegiance to at least two sovereigns. One is the United States, and the other is their state. They can therefore potentially commit treason against either, or against both.

Levying war means the assembly of armed people to overthrow the government or to resist its laws.

Any person convicted of treason against the United States will lose the right to hold public office in the United States.]

January 30 - On January 6, thousands of predominantly white, right-wing fanatics swarmed the US Capitol, ransacking offices and hunting down lawmakers and the sitting vice president as they revolted against the results of a free and fair election.

The event was a stunning window into the violent and racist ideology that had bubbled under the surface for decades before exploding into the open after its supporters were fed a steady diet of lies and disinformation by a president who was angry over his election loss. Now, many insurrectionists are facing federal charges and former President Donald Trump is staring down a second impeachment and potential criminal prosecution.

Frank Montoya, Jr., a recently retired FBI special agent, told Insider that the Capitol siege indicates far-right extremism is a 'fundamental' threat to national security, even more so than foreign terror groups. Indeed, many of these extremists are white, male US citizens, some with backgrounds in the military, and are less likely to be profiled as a terror threat than those of Middle Eastern descent in the post-9/11 era.

"The threat we're facing right now is not only real - but deeply embedded and cult-like in our society," Montoya said. "Look at how many military and law enforcement types were involved in the Capitol assault and how many people in Congress supported the effort to overturn a free and fair election on January 6."

"If the attack had come from ISIS or Al-Qaeda, there would be blue-ribbon commissions, legislation, billions of dollars and thousands of employees from across the government thrown at the problem," he added. "The First Amendment and civil liberties are paramount, but far-right extremism isn't about that. It's about insurrection."

The Department of Homeland Security issued an advisory this week warning of a 'heightened threat environment across the United States which DHS believes will persist in the weeks following the Presidential Inauguration.'

"Information suggests that some ideologically-motivated violent extremists with objections to the exercise of governmental authority and the presidential transition, as well as other perceived grievances fuelled by false narratives, could continue to mobilize to incite or commit violence," the advisory said, adding that the DHS expects these threats to persist through early 2021.

January 29 - A law firm that formerly represented the Trump Organisation has been ordered to hand over documents to a New York Attorney General investigating the former president.

Letitia James' investigation into the organization's finances and Trump's personal finances aims to determine if the Trump Organisation falsely inflated the value of Trump's assets to get access to loans and tax benefits. The law firm that previously worked for the organisation, Morgan, Lewis & Bockius, had argued that the documents were protected by attorney-client privilege. But as it concerned business, not legal advice, Justice Arthur Engoron said that they weren't protected, the agency reported.

"A lawyer's communication is not cloaked with privilege when the lawyer is hired for business or personal advice, or to do the work of a nonlawyer."

- The US Center for Disease Control (CDC) issued a far-reaching set of orders that dramatically expands the federal mask mandate.

Starting February 2, all passengers in the US are required to mask up on any form of public transit: ferries, trains, buses, taxis, and rideshares like Uber or Lyft. Airlines and other transit operators are required to remove passengers who don't comply.

The mandate follows a Biden executive order mandating masks for interstate travel, but it expands the scope even to shorter-distance trips like subways or city buses. The order was exactly what the Trump administration previously forbade the CDC from doing, in a failure to act which likely cost untold numbers of lives.

February 2 - The clock is ticking towards former US president Donald Trump's second impeachment trial. Last week, a team of Democratic impeachment managers delivered the article of impeachment to the Senate, formalising the beginning of the trial process, but there are still a few steps to get through before the trial actually begins, and one of those is almost due.

A summons would have been issued to Mr. Trump after the House delivered the impeachment article to the Senate last week. Senate Republican leader Mitch McConnell announced on January 21 that Mr. Trump would have one week from the day the article was sent to the Senate to answer the article of impeachment.

Today is the deadline for Mr. Trump to respond to the article of impeachment. Based on his previous remarks, it seems Mr. Trump is unlikely to concede to any wrongdoing. In the past he's called this latest impeachment a 'continuation of the greatest witch hunt in the history of politics.'

Whichever tack defence lawyers take, the 100 Democratic and Republican senators who will serve as jurors are anticipating the trial may only run for a few days. This would be far shorter than Trump's first trial, which lasted three weeks.

Mr. Trump's pre-trial brief is due next Monday, February 8 local time, as is the House's response to Mr. Trump's answer.

The House's pre-trial rebuttal brief, which lays out the case against Mr. Trump, is due the next day. Once this is filed, the trial can officially begin. It's not clear exactly how long the trial itself will be.

The House is also likely to indicate today whether they plan to call witnesses. This was a flash point in the first impeachment trial when Republicans blocked witness testimony or the introduction of additional evidence against Mr. Trump.

- Today, former President **Donald Trump** found a new outlet to air his unfounded claims about voter fraud, using his legal response to impeachment charges against him in the US Congress as a vehicle for his conspiracy theory.

Trump's desire to use the Senate impeachment trial to air his fraud claims was a factor in his parting of ways with five lawyers over the weekend, who wanted to focus on constitutional questions, a source familiar with the situation said.

His answer to the House impeachment case is dominated by the constitutional argument that a former president cannot be impeached.

But the Trump argument, issued through his new lawyers, Bruce Castor and David Schoen, does stray into voter fraud territory, despite pleas from US Senator John Cornyn of Texas that Trump's defence not 'get bogged down in things that really aren't before the Senate.'

The Trump legal response said Trump, who had used speeches and tweets to claim the election was stolen from him, had exercised 'his First Amendment right under the Constitution to express his belief that the election results were suspect.'

Trump, who had railed against mail-in voting prior to the election, said in his impeachment response that due to coronavirus pandemic safeguards, state election laws and procedures were changed by local politicians or judges without approval from state legislatures.

On February 4, Democratic impeachment manager Jamie Raskin, called on Mr. Trump to appear as a witness at the Senate trial starting on February 9th, with claims he incited an insurrection on the Capitol. The request laid down a challenge to the ex-president, who was not subpoenaed to testify, as expected. His lawyers denounced the request as a 'public relations stunt.'

Mr. Trump, responding to the request through adviser Jason Miller, separately called the process 'unconstitutional.'

February 7 - After refusing to testify at his Senate impeachment trial, Donald Trump has walked right into a 'constitutional jiu jitsu' trap set up by Democrats who want to convict him with the former president risking a future criminal trial.

February 9 – **The Impeachment Trial of Donald Trump** will be tried in the Senate for a second time. When proceedings against the single-term US president start today. The trial comes almost a month after Congress was besieged by his supporters, who wrongly claimed that last year's election was 'stolen' or 'rigged' after Mr. Trump lost to Democrat Joe Biden.

Democrats – and some Republicans - afterwards said Mr. Trump, who pushed those allegations in the months leading up to the attack on the Capitol, 'incited' that very 'insurrection' on 6 January,2021.

Following his impeachment by the House on 13 January, a single article of impeachment was passed to the Senate on 25 January, paving the way for the trial to start two weeks later. Mr. Trump in January became the first ever president in US history to be impeached twice.

The Senate trial starts today, under plans agreed to by the chamber's Democratic and Republican leaders, Chuck Schumer and Mitch McConnell. Senators will convene around midday to begin proceedings, at which point impeachment managers – appointed by House Speaker Nancy Pelosi – will start presenting their case.

The impeachment managers, who are led by Maryland Representative Jamie Raskin, are expected to take several days to set out their argument, with the segment concluding around 10 or 11 February.

The eight Democrats will release an 80-page brief outlining their position, alleging the former president's public actions and 'singular responsibility for that tragedy' that occurred on 6 January.

Mr. Trump's lawyers were required to outline their arguments and published a fourteen-page brief that incorrectly spelled 'United States' in the opening lines and argued for 'free speech.'

Though a final schedule has not been released, both parties are likely to agree to pause the trial over the weekend to allow for one of Mr. Trump's lawyers, David Schoen, to observe the Sabbath. Both parties appear to be aiming for a week-long trial.

After the impeachment managers have made their arguments to the Senate, the former US president's lawyers will mount a verbal counter argument to allegations he caused the Capitol riot. While they will have the same time as the impeachment managers to present to the Senate, it is not clear whether or not there will be an opportunity to object to points already made by the managers. Senate president pro tempore Patrick Leahy, who will preside over the trial, would rule on, or allow, senators to debate Mr. Trump's lawyer's objections – which could take some time.

After both sides set-out arguments, attention turns to senators themselves, who will act as jurors in the trial. Senators will send arguments in written form to Senator Leahy, who will direct questions to the impeachment managers or Mr. Trump's lawyers.

They had only 16 hours to do so when Mr. Trump faced his first impeachment trial in January 2020, and this time around, that point could come sometime around 15 or 16 February.

Four hours will also be set aside today for debate over the constitutionality of the impeachment hearings. Republican Senators have argued that the trial is unconstitutional because a former president cannot be impeached. Democrats, many constitutional scholars, and some Republicans disagree with that interpretation.

The Senate will then decide whether they will call on witnesses and documents, with a debate preceding a vote on whether to do so.

Democrats, who hold the deciding vote in the Senate, will be expected to win a vote on calling witnesses, and will begin tabling motions to subpoena them, to support their arguments against Mr. Trump. The former president's lawyers would in this case also be expected to call on witnesses to support their defence.

While Mr. Trump's previous impeachment trial took three weeks, this trial could be shorter after a majority of Republicans recently voted to dismiss the trial outright. The vote, which did not pass, was still a sign that the Senate will not vote by the two-thirds (or 67 votes) needed to convict the former president.

The argument that Mr. Trump 'incited' the mob who attacked Congress is also publicly evident – and so will be expected to take less time debating. Following a vote on whether to convict the former president, the Senate will then likely vote separately barring Mr. Trump from holding future office. This will require only majority support.

February 9 - The first day of former President Trump's second Senate impeachment trial opened with a video. As the full video reached its end, Lead House Impeachment Manager Jamie Raskin (D-MD) pointed to the screen and said, "If that is not an impeachable offense, then there is no such thing."

Raskin, whose son died days before the insurrection, closed with an emotional description of the events on January 6th. In one particularly hard-hitting moment, Raskin cried when he spoke about his daughter not wanting to come back to the Capitol after she had to hide during the violence.

The video - which essentially made the entire case for conviction - was how House impeachment managers started their presentation.

Representative Raskin began the House's presentation, arguing that if the Senate grants a 'January exception' to presidential misconduct by letting Trump off the hook, they will invite future post-presidency corruption. Then Impeachment Manager Joe Neguse dove into the precedents of impeaching former officials, with the examples of William Blount and William Belknap.

Then Bruce Castor stood up, and things took a strange turn. He openly admitted that he'd had to pivot after hearing the House Impeachment Managers' presentation. Castor's "pivot" appeared more like he was filibustering his own time to give his team space to prepare. Trump's lawyer, David Schoen, made an ineffective effort to save the case. They claimed that the impeachment process was somehow simultaneously too speedy and delayed. They blamed the delay of the trial on Speaker Nancy Pelosi (D-CA) rather than McConnell, who had refused to convene the Senate for an emergency session. The logic - and the delivery - was difficult to follow.

Even Senator John Cornyn (R-TX) acknowledged, "The president's lawyer just rambled on and on... I've seen a lot of lawyers and a lot of arguments and that was not one of the finest I've seen." Cornyn still voted in favour of the Trump team's argument.

Most legal experts agree that this Senate impeachment trial is indeed constitutional. House managers cited multiple conservatives who hold that opinion, including co-founder of the Federalist Society Steven Calabresi, Judge Michael McConnell, and prominent conservative lawyer Charles Cooper spoke, and had detailed his reasoning two days earlier in the Wall Street Journal.

Most Senate Republicans were not swayed. At the end of the day, forty-four Senate Republicans voted 'no' on the constitutionality of the trial with only Senator Bill Cassidy (R-LA) changing his mind and voting with Democrats. The 'no' votes included Senate Minority Leader Mitch McConnell (R-KY). Such an outcome highlighted the complete lack of seriousness with which Trump's legal team, and apparently 44 Senate Republicans, are taking this trial.

It's unclear whether all 44 Republicans who voted 'no' today will also vote 'no' on conviction, but their actions do send a clear signal of where their heads are at. These votes show it doesn't matter how effective the House arguments are. Trump's lawyers utterly failed, as admitted by pretty much everyone in session, and yet we have this result.

As the trial progresses, we'll see if more Senate Republicans change their mind or if the fix is in for Trump to get away with his part in the insurrection.

February 14 – - US approves Johnson and Johnson one-dose vaccine.

- The Senate **acquitted** former President Donald Trump a second time after a historic trial where House managers painted him as a lingering threat after his supporters led a deadly riot in the Capitol Jan. 6, but Republican senators found the effort unnecessary for a president no longer in office. A 57-43 majority of the Senate voted to convict Trump but fell short of the two-thirds majority required for conviction. Seven Republicans joined the 50 lawmakers who caucus with Democrats. Trump was also acquitted a year ago in his first trial about his dealings with Ukraine, when a majority opposed conviction and only one Republican joined Democrats voting to convict.

While the acquittal was expected, it will stand for generations as an appalling instance of Republican Party cowardice. It demonstrates how intrinsically bound the party's fortunes remain to Mr. Trump and his followers.

[I feel the need to repeat what I said earlier: Not only should Trump be convicted of *impeachment* – he should also be charged with *treason* because he incited radical American terrorists to overthrow the legally elected government.

The definition of Treason in the United States is:

Treason: the crime of betraying one's country. Constitutionally, citizens of the United States owe allegiance to at least two sovereigns. One is the United States, and the other is their state. They can therefore potentially commit treason against either, or against both.

Levying war means the assembly of armed people to overthrow the government or to resist its laws.

Any person convicted of treason against the United States will lose the right to hold public office in the United States.]

"History is not there for you to like or dislike. It is there for you to learn from it. And if it offends you, even better, because then you are less likely to repeat it. It's not yours to erase. It belongs to all of us." **Anonymous**

CHAPTER 5

AUSTRALIAN GOVERNMENT ACTION

One hundred years ago, on January 28, 1919 **Queensland** closed its borders for the first time in history. Barricades were swiftly placed between Tweed Heads and Coolangatta. Train passengers who were holidaying in NSW couldn't get back to Queensland. Border camps were established. More than 800 travellers were stranded at Tenterfield. Many returned to Sydney to go by steamer to Brisbane. As is happening now, people were willing to sneak across the border. They were segregated from others. To enter at the border, they had to go in isolation for at least seven days. They were inoculated with pneumonic-influenza vaccine.

By May 17 preparations were being made to open the Queensland border. The residents celebrated. The flu epidemic officially arrived in Queensland on May 23, when two women were the first to be diagnosed. It quickly spread.

August 9 2020 - **Canberra** – Prime Minister **Scott Morrison** has stated that any vaccine that is invented must be shared internationally. Countries that do not do this will be dealt with very harshly.

August 10 - The states of **New South Wales (NSW)** and the **Australian Capital Territory (ACT**) and **Victoria** are all declared COVID-19 hotspots.

Since 1:00 am on Saturday, August 8, the **Queensland** border has been closed to anyone who has been in a COVID-19 hotspot in the last 14 days unless they receive an exemption.

Residents living in the declared 'border zone' will be able to apply for a new declaration border pass but will only be permitted to travel within the border zone in Queensland and New South Wales.

Queensland residents who have been in a COVID-19 hotspot can return home via air but will be required to quarantine for 14 days in government arranged accommodation at their own expense.

Anyone entering Queensland cannot travel by road through a COVID-19 hotspot (New South Wales) and must arrange to travel by air unless an exception has been granted.

The new Queensland Border Declaration Pass is a requirement for anyone entering Queensland by road, air or sea and includes returning Queensland residents.

The new Queensland Border Declaration Passes consist of the following categories:

X PASS: Border zone resident, issued to persons living in a border zone who are not required to quarantine.

G PASS: General, issued to a Queensland resident or interstate visitors who are allowed to enter Queensland and are not subject to a quarantine direction. This pass cannot be used at a New South Wales road border.

S PASS: Specialist, issued to exempt persons who have been to a COVID-19 declared hotspot and are not required to quarantine.

F PASS: Freight, issued to freight, logistics and transport workers who are not required to quarantine.

Q PASS: Quarantine Direction, issued to a person who is allowed to enter Queensland but must quarantine.

Providing false information on the declaration or entering Queensland unlawfully could result in a $4,003 fine or a notice to appear in court. Queensland government is warning that if more people risk coming illegally into Queensland, the border will be closed to everyone.

August 13 - From 9:00 am today until August 17, **ACT** residents in **Victoria** will also be permitted to drive through **NSW** to return to **Canberra**, however they were ordered not to stop until they reached the **ACT.**

 - **New South Wales** government has granted a one-month grace period for residents stranded in **Victoria** and allows them time to return home without having to pay for mandatory hotel quarantine.

August 19 - Prime Minister Scott Morrison is encouraging Australians to get the COVID-19 vaccination as soon as it is available.

Coronavirus vaccine dodgers could lose government payments, Health Minister Greg Hunt said. Australians who choose not to be vaccinated against coronavirus could lose access to welfare payments, Greg Hunt said, after the Prime Minister conceded vaccination would not be mandatory. He added that if a vaccine was discovered, the Government would consider applying measures like "no jab, no pay" to ensure a high uptake.

The government will aim for a 95 per cent vaccination rate, which it said would exclude those who cannot take the shot on medical grounds.

August 23 – An outbreak of coronavirus has closed the set of the TV show The Masked Singer that is filmed at the Melbourne Docklands studio. One of the dancers felt ill on August 21st and was tested. Close contacts of the dancer were tested, and several were positive. The stars have been told to self-isolate.

New Restrictions

- **Queensland** - Brisbane City, Ipswich City, Logan City, Scenic Rim, Somerset Region, Lockyer Valley, Moreton Bayh and Redland City (affecting approximately 3 million people):

- 10 people maximum at gatherings in homes and areas without COVID Safe Plans.
- Aged care and disability services closed to visitors

 - The rest of Queensland:

- 30 people maximum in homes and areas without COVID Safe Plans
- This is indefinite but will be reviewed in two weeks.

August 23 - **Australia** – has had 300 deaths in Aged Care Centres.

August 29 – **Denmark** is helping Australia develop a new system to define COVID-19 hotspots which would lock down those regions and allow state borders to re-open. The new system would likely be based on a traffic light system used in Denmark which would see travel bans introduced to regions with high numbers of cases. In Denmark, a region is considered safe if there are fewer than 20 cases per 100,000 inhabitants over a week.

Doctors are struggling trying to keep their patients safe. The Australian Medical Association Queensland president Chris Perry said he had spent $13,000 on masks and gowns for his patients and staff since March. Since then, the N95 respirator mask soared from

$1.00 per mask to $6.00 per mask and from $.20 for a surgical mask to $1.00.

September 1 - The **Australian Taxation Office** (ATO) has now issued preliminary guidance on the extension of the JobKeeper stimulus measure to 28 March 2021, following its passage through Parliament on 1 September. The Coronavirus Economic Response Package (Jobkeeper Payments) Amendment Bill 2020 was passed by Senate today, extending the government's wage subsidy program by six months to 28 March 2021.

Under the new regulation, JobKeeper 2.0 will replace the current flat $1,500 a fortnight subsidy with a two-tiered system.

The subsidy will consist of a $750 fortnightly payment for those working under 20 hours pre-COVID and $1,200 per fortnight for others. This will then be reduced further from January next year to $650 and $1,000, respectively.

According to the guidance, businesses already enrolled in JobKeeper will not need to re-enrol nor will they need to reassess employee eligibility or ask employees to agree to be nominated, but they will need to determine if they satisfy the actual fall in turnover test for the two extension periods:

The first extension period begins from 28 September 2020 to 3 January 2021.

The second extension period begins from 4 January 2021 to 28 March 2021.

As of 4 January, these payment rates will decrease further to $1,000 and $650 per fortnight.

September 4 – **Australia** – 87 new cases – 59 deaths.

Between March 14 and September 5th there were 607,000 private sector job losses. This averaged 3,500 were unemployed per day in Australia. The majority of new jobs created since May are part-time only. 70% of job losses were for workers who were under 35 years of age. Australian Retailers Association head Paul Zahara said that, "People who are unskilled or semi-skilled are really going to struggle through the 2020s."

September 6 – Queensland is awaiting the approval of a multibillion-dollar pipeline of projects. The 22 proposed projects would create nearly 20,000 jobs

September 8 – total deaths in Australia now 762.

September 9 - Health experts have urged Australians not to be concerned about the safety and progress of the Oxford coronavirus vaccine after phase three trials were halted. British drug producer AstraZeneca and Oxford University voluntarily suspended the late-stage tests after a participant experienced an 'adverse reaction.'

In its statement, AstraZeneca said the pause was a 'routine action.' to allow an independent investigation into the 'potentially unexplained illness,' in one of its participants.

"This is a routine action which has to happen whenever there is an unexplained illness in one of the trials, while it is investigated, ensuring we maintain the integrity of the trials," the company said.

"In large trials illnesses will happen by chance but must be independently reviewed to check this carefully."

Australia's Deputy Chief Medical Officer Nick Coatsworth said it was far too soon to draw a link between the vaccine and the condition.

"I think one of the most important things is to remember that many thousands of cases of transverse myelitis would occur in Australia and around the world every year that have nothing to do with vaccines," he said.

"With many thousands of people getting the vaccine, medical events can happen that have nothing to do with a vaccine."

September 13 – In May, Australian Federal Police raided a Canberra apartment block that housed Chinese embassy staff. Tensions were escalating between Canberra and Beijing. Attorney-General Christian Porter refused to comment on this operational or national security matter.

September 18 – Returning Australians - There are an estimated 25,000 stranded Australians wanting to return home which the government has pledged to facilitate before Christmas.

Australia closed its international borders early in the coronavirus pandemic, and imposed strict lockdowns and social distancing measures, dramatically reducing the spread of coronavirus.

Health Minister Greg Hunt says that states can 'absolutely' handle a significantly larger load of returning Australians in hotel quarantine as National Cabinet prepares to discuss boosting the intake from 4,000 to 6,000 per week.

He said former secretary of the Finance Department Jane Halton finished her 'top-to-bottom' review of the states' hotel quarantine systems and returned an 'overwhelmingly a positive assessment.'

"Because of the concerns about **Victoria,** we lost the Victorian capacity and some of the states wound back some of their capacity just to make sure that they were safe. If we can bring home Australians, of course we should bring them home."

Western Australia and Queensland have argued it's not their responsibility to support overseas travel.

As the country's number of infections slow, Queensland state said that it would open its border to residents of Canberra, which has had no new infections in ten weeks.

Queensland has not registered any local infections in eight days, its deputy premier Steven Miles said.

"Now for people from Canberra, Queensland is good to come. Now is the time and we urge them to start thinking to come up to Queensland for a holiday."

September 25 - **Queensland** will allow 152,000 more people living along the state's southern border to enter, as South Australia also moves to ease restrictions for New South Wales travellers.

South Australia's Chief Public Health Officer Nicola Spurrier said zero community transmission in NSW for 14 days had prompted the decision to reopen.

Meanwhile, Queensland's Chief Health Officer Jeannette Young said if there continued to be very low or no new cases in the state's southern neighbour, restrictions could be further relaxed from today.

From today, you can travel to **Queensland** from **ACT** if no new cases emerge in the ACT before then. You won't have to quarantine when you arrive in Queensland, as long as you haven't been through a COVID-19 hotspot in the fortnight preceding your arrival.

For those travelling to the nation's capital, there are directions to be followed if you have recently been in Victoria or some areas of Greater Sydney or Queensland. Travellers are asked to not visit or work in high-risk settings, like hospitals, aged care homes, and correctional facilities for 14 days after arriving.

From October 1, people living in 41 more **New South Wales** postcodes will be able to apply for a border pass to travel into **Queensland**. Residents in Byron Bay, Ballina, Lismore, Richmond Valley and Glen Innes local government areas are the most recent areas to be added to the zone, which extends as far south as Moree. Queensland residents will also be able to travel to those areas.

The changes come after Queensland recorded zero new coronavirus cases overnight, leaving just 16 active cases.

In **NSW**, September 22 was the first time in more than 70 days no new locally acquired cases were found.

Travellers can go from **NSW** to **ACT** to **Queensland**, but they will have to quarantine once they arrive in Queensland. Unless they've gone from a NSW border zone area to the ACT without going through any other part of NSW, which is probably only possible by aircraft.

ACT travellers will have to fill out a border declaration form, confirming they haven't been in NSW or Victoria, to enter Queensland.

South Australia will reopen its borders to **NSW** at midnight today, as long as there is no community transmission of coronavirus reported in NSW today. As well as being able to enter SA, NSW residents will no longer have to quarantine for 14 days. If they're travelling into SA, they'll still be required to complete an online approval form.

People in self-isolation after entering from NSW will have to finish their fortnight's quarantine.

If they're in **Victoria**, they can only enter SA if they are an essential traveller or live within 40 kilometres of the SA border.

Unfortunately, residents of **Victoria** are still not allowed to travel to other states and territories unless they meet one of three criteria - holding an exemption, being an essential worker or living along a state border. Even then, those granted access to NSW under a border region resident permit cannot go further into the state than the border region.

"You'll need to apply for a NSW resident's permit to re-enter NSW (requiring a flight to Sydney Airport and quarantine)," the NSW Government said.

Victoria's Department of Health and Human Services website reads: "No permit or approval is required to enter Victoria from another state - however, you will need to adhere to the restrictions and directions that are in place to slow the spread of coronavirus in Victoria."

Western Australia - Exempt travellers include Commonwealth workers, truck drivers, emergency service workers, federal politicians and dependents. Transport and freight workers will have to prove they have tested negative to COVID-19 in the five days prior to their arrival. Everyone else has to quarantine for 14 days before they'll be allowed to move about in the state freely.

And if they're planning to travel from **Victoria** or **NSW** to **WA**, they won't be allowed in without written approval from the state emergency coordinator.

In **Tasmania** there are some exemptions for seasonal and FIFO workers. Otherwise, the Tasmanian Government will consider bringing forward the date for easing coronavirus border restrictions to the end of October. Premier Peter Gutwein said if controls were relaxed, travellers from WA, SA, QLD the NT, ACT, and possibly NSW, may be able to visit, but that depends on advice from the state controller, which is expected over the coming weeks.

September 29 - **Australia** now has had 27,000 cases (Victoria had 75% of these cases. Total deaths – 886 – Victoria had 90% of these.)

October 10 - **Victorian** Premier Daniel Andrews has announced that he has extended the State of Emergency and the State of Disaster by another four weeks.

"I've just signed paperwork to extend the state of emergency and the state of disaster from tonight to 11:59 pm on November 8," Mr. Andrews said.

"That is simply to make sure that we've got that legal framework in place in order to continue to have rules, to drive these numbers down even further.

October 15 – **Australia** - Doctors treating people with long-term symptoms of COVID-19 will need to closely monitor patients for potential heart or lung disease, according to a new guide for Australian GPs released today.

A new guide for Australian GPs urges them to create a treatment plan with patients who have long term symptoms from COVID-19. It is estimated 80 per cent of people who require hospitalisation with COVID-19 will experience post-COVID-19 symptoms.

The Royal Australian College of General Practitioners has proposed a Medicare subsidy for people who have long-term symptoms to support longer consultations.

The guide, released by the Royal Australian College of General Practitioners (RACGP), says common long-term symptoms that will require treatment include fatigue, shortness of breath and chest pain, as well as rarer, more severe conditions such as heart and lung damage, stroke and neurological decline.

October 19 - **Australian** researchers have designed a 15-minute COVID-19 test which could provide a silver bullet for the country's internal travel and border woes. The University of Technology Sydney scientists say they have developed a sensitive saliva test which can pick up SARS-CoV-2 viral fragments in less than 15 minutes.

With a hard border in place in Western Australia and travel restrictions of varying severity implemented across Australia's other states, the researchers say rapid COVID-19 testing could boost virus detection and help in the screening of travellers. It could also be useful in hospital, aged care and employment settings.

The test prototype will be manufactured in Perth and would cost less than $25 per test. Laboratory trials on live virus are expected to begin before Christmas.

October 26 - **Victoria** has been in lockdown for 85 days – since June 9th. Today, Victoria recorded no new COVID-19 cases or deaths for the first time since then.

Melbourne residents head into their final day of lockdown, with many of the city's tough restrictions eased from 11.59 pm tonight.

- **Tasmania** will ease border restrictions for people travelling from Queensland, the Australian Capital Territory, South Australia, Western Australia and the Northern Territory without quarantining. The situation is continuing to be monitored in NSW.

It will be relatively easy for Tasmanians to travel to these states and territory and the ACT, and then return home.

Tasmania is open to Western Australia, but WAQ has a hard border, meaning that Tasmanians won't be able to go there unless they have an exemption. To enter the states and territories that are open, Tasmanians may need to fill out a border entry form ahead of time, and check their travel route, because jurisdictions have different rules about travelling through hotspots.

For example, travellers intending to enter South Australia need to complete a Cross Border Travel Registration and must not transit via a Victorian airport to enter the state.

Queensland considers Victoria and New South Wales COVID-19 hotspots, but travellers who have had a flight layover in a hotspot are allowed to enter Queensland, as long as they can provide evidence that they were only in the hotspot to transfer flights and didn't leave the airport.

October 30 - New Protocol in **Queensland.** Here's what changed from 3:00 pm today:

- Increase the validity of the Border Declaration Pass from 7 to 14 days.
- Allow unaccompanied minors to enter Queensland if there is a responsible adult who consents to quarantine in government arranged accommodation with the child.

- Allow disaster management workers to enter Queensland to prepare for, respond to or assist in recovery from disasters.
- Give effect to the new Disaster Management Protocol.
- Include new requirements for how people can travel to quarantine or leave quarantine for permitted purposes such as that a person travelling in a taxi must travel in the back seat on the passenger side.
- Require people in quarantine to wear a mask whenever directed to by an emergency officer.
- Not allow people who are waiting for the results of a COVID-19 test to enter Queensland until they receive a negative result, unless they are entering for an essential activity.
- To clarify that as soon as a place is removed from the list of COVID-19 hotspot, you can enter Queensland even if you had been to that place in the 14 days before.
- Include 3 new postcodes in the border zone. These are Queensland postcodes that extend into New South Wales: 4375, 4377 and 4380.

November 11 - Australians are being warned the Pfizer vaccine may take longer than expected and the required two shots means it would cover only five million people here.

November 22 – A breakthrough Australian nasal spray that not only stops coronavirus but also prevents the common cold and influenza has been given government funding to commence human trials. In September trials done on ferrets showed it was 96% effective at preventing the replication of the virus that causes COVID-19 in the nose. It will now be taken to the next stage for testing in Sydney in December and other trials will begin in March 2021.

November 29 – **Australia** - New security safety measures will force all passengers and crew to return a negative COVID-19 test before they can board cruise ships with regular on-board testing. The sector hopes they will see cruising return by Christmas. Only ships with fewer than 100 passengers are permitted to enter Australian waters.

November 30 – **JobKeeper** – The number of people relying on JobKeeper payments declined by almost 34,000 from October to November which the federal government says is a sign that the economy is recovering.

December 4 - **NSW**'s 25-day virus-free streak has come to an end and you can sense the buoyancy evaporating as instantly as Gladys Berejiklian's long overdue holiday.

A woman working between two Sydney hotels – one for quarantined returned travellers – and travelling to and from work on two rail systems, shows how vulnerable we are if we don't learn from previous mistakes.

As the Premier calls the situation 'very serious' and contact tracers scramble to alert those who came into contact with the woman either at the Ibis or Novotel hotels, or on public transport. There's incredulity that a critical frontline worker could work between a quarantine hotel and one simply serving members of the public.

Hotel quarantine is like a Petri dish for the virus. Mismanage even the slightest factor and suddenly deaths can skyrocket, borders can again slam shut, and ordinary lives can be brought to a standstill.

December 8 - **Western Australia** will reopen to NSW and Victoria today after being closed to the states for nearly nine months.

The border softening will see many reunited in time for Christmas however travellers from South Australia will not be included in the new eased restrictions and will have to wait longer before being allowed free access to the state.

December 20 – **Sydney** has had another breakout of the virus. Other states have ordered that anyone who has been in the Northern Beaches area since December 11 will need to self-quarantine for 14 days if they come to their state.

- **Queensland** – Border passes have been reintroduced and hundreds of thousands of Queenslanders are being urged to get tested for coronavirus as a precaution that they might have been exposed to 11 people linked to the Sydney outbreak who are now in Queensland.

International flight crews have been ordered into government-run hotel quarantine and Gold Coast police began a border blitz on NSW vehicles.

December 22 - **Queensland** border checkpoints have been reinstated at all major border crossings and will be continually rolled out across the state by 6:00 am today. Anyone entering

Queensland by road or air from New South Wales, including Queensland residents will need to complete a border declaration pass online prior to travelling to Queensland. Providing false information on the declaration or entering Queensland unlawfully could result in a $4,003 fine.

Those who have travelled from a declared New South Wales hotspot on or since Friday, December 11 are urged to get a COVID-19 test and immediately self-isolate. Travellers are also directed to apply for a Queensland border direction pass.

Queensland residents returning from a hotspot before 1:00 am today are able to complete a 14-day quarantine process at home, provided they undergo a COVID-19 test. People quarantining at a private address need to take their obligations seriously and stay at home.

Police will be conducting random checks on those people in home quarantine to ensure they are doing the right thing and not putting others at risk by going into public spaces.

A police presence will remain at airports with compliance checks carried out on all flights from New South Wales and random checks on passengers disembarking from other interstate flights.

January 24 – Doctors throughout Australia will bulk bill COVID-1 vaccines through Medicare. The Pfizer vaccine will be delivered to hospitals due to the stringent storage refrigeration requirements. GPs will be mostly responsible for administering up to 53 million doses of the AstraZeneca vaccine. Both vaccines require two shots within 21 days.

But who will go first? Australia's vaccination program will hopefully prioritise the over-80s, care home residents, frontline health and case workers, and those deemed extremely vulnerable. Next in line would likely be the over-65s and people with risky conditions such as diabetes. About 75% of deaths worldwide are people over 65 and many hospitals have refused to treat or revive elderly sufferers.

January 25 - The nation's medical regulator the Therapeutic Goods Administration has approved Pfizer's COVID-19 vaccine and Australia has purchased 10 million doses of the vaccine.

The TGA said following a thorough and independent review of Pfizer's submission, it was decided the vaccine met the high safety, efficacy and quality standards required. It is the first COVID-19 vaccine to be approved for use in Australia. The approval is on a provisional basis, meaning it is valid for two years. It allows the vaccine to be supplied in Australia for people aged 16 and older. Two doses will be required at least 21 days apart. COVID-19 vaccine will not be mandatory.

Prime Minister Scott Morrison welcomed the decision. "Australians should take confidence in the thorough and careful approach taken by our world-class safety regulator," he said.

"Our priority has always been to keep Australians safe and protect lives and livelihoods. Today's approval is another big step forward for our community, particularly in the protection of our most vulnerable people."

The Government wants to start rolling out the vaccine in February, prioritising groups such as healthcare workers and Australians in aged care homes.

Minister for Health Greg Hunt said, "This approval and the upcoming rollout of the vaccine will play an important part in our ability to manage the pandemic in 2021."

The TGA said it would continue to monitor the safety of the Pfizer vaccine both in Australia and overseas and 'will not hesitate to take action if safety concerns are identified.'

January 31 – Victoria, NSW and now Queensland authorities will be empowered to give on-the-spot fines of $200 to anyone who flouts wearing a mask when asked to do so by public health directives. And anyone caught breaching any other aspect of public health directions beyond mask mandates could still be fined $1,334.

– **Queensland** – Help for the unemployed: Springfield City Group, one of Queensland's most prominent land developers, has unveiled a five-year plan to create 20,000 jobs and transform 42ha in Springfield into a twelve-billion-dollar new 'Internet City.' The site will be called IDEA (Innovation, Design, Entrepreneurship and Arts).

ENGIE, a world leader in the global transition to clean, green resilient economies has devised a three-billion-dollar plan which aims to make Springfield the world's most eco-friendly community by 2038.

February 2 – Australia - The much-anticipated COVID-19 vaccine is almost ready to be rolled out across Australia, but with its arrival comes an array of questions.

The first to receive the vaccine will be anyone who lives or works in aged care, hotel quarantine or frontline health with vaccinations likely to begin this month. Adults under 50 who are not essential workers or in high-risk settings will be last in line for the provisionally approved Pfizer vaccine. Children are not yet able to receive the vaccine and it is not recommended for pregnant women.

Pfizer's vaccine is the only one so far approved for use here in Australia with about 10 million doses ordered, which presents a problem as everyone needs two vaccines at least three weeks apart.

This means that about five million Australians will be covered, so much of the general population is unlikely to get the Pfizer vaccine. Most Australians will instead get the Oxford-AstraZeneca vaccine, which is being made in Melbourne for a deal of more than 50 million doses.

Speculation around the safety of the vaccine has been rife, but the Therapeutic Goods Administration (TGA) say it is safe and will be carrying out testing and monitoring throughout the rollout. The side effects of the vaccine are understood to be short term and much like the flu vaccine. People may feel fatigued or be prone to headaches and more than a third will have muscle pain and chills, while joint pain is also possible but less likely.

The Federal Government is hoping to have most - if not the entire population vaccinated by October at no cost to recipients.

February 14 – **Queensland** – 1,500 travellers who entered Queensland on February 9th have been put into isolation after possibly being exposed to a highly infectious strain of COVID-19 at Melbourne's Tullamarine Airport.

CHAPTER 6

AUSTRALIA DURING PANDEMIC

August 8 – **Victoria** - 416 new cases today – 12 deaths.

- **NSW** - 11 new cases.

- **Queensland** – A new trial is coming for patients who have had Covid-19 which will help them in their recovery. They will be given an anti-viral injection during the first 5 days of infection. They're asking for volunteers.

Fourteen million Australian people are now banned from Queensland. There were cars queued for many kilometres yesterday of people wishing to beat the border deadline of 1:00 a.m. today. Passes were not available. Only Tweed Head residents were allowed in as well as transport and emergency services workers. NSW construction workers may be given passes to work on construction sites in Queensland.

- Dream World and Movie World are scheduled to open next month.

- Organisers for the planned Story Bridge protest in Brisbane have postponed the protest for one week after threats of mass arrests over fight for refugee rights.

August 9 - **Victoria** has recorded its deadliest day of the pandemic, with 17 more fatalities across the state and 394 new cases.

The previous highest daily death toll was 15 fatalities on August 5. Ten of the 17 deaths have been linked to outbreaks in aged care.

Police handed out 268 fines for breaking COVID-19 health restrictions, which included 38 fines for failing to wear a face covering, 13 fines at vehicle checkpoints and 77 fines for breaching curfew.

- **NSW** - Ten new cases of COVID-19 were diagnosed in the 24 hours to 8:00 pm last night, bringing the total number of cases in NSW to 3,672.

August 10 – - **Victoria** – 322 new cases – 19 deaths.

- **Queensland** – Patterson Community College re-opens. No new cases in Queensland. Aged Care Homes now open again in Queensland.

A suite of new border declaration passes for those eligible to enter Queensland are available online.

August 10 – At the Wacol Detention Centre, a supervisor, aged 77 who was from Bundamba developed symptoms today and tested positive on August 19.

- That same day a male **Youth Detention Centre Worker** who lived in Marsden and tested positive for the virus. Another male and his partner from that centre who lived in Carindale had been working at the Springwood State High School before he tested positive.

August 11 – **Melbourne** – A guard for hotel quarantine facilities choked a 21-year-old for not wearing a mask. 331 new cases with 19 deaths.

- **Queensland** – 2 teenagers illegally crossed the border – negative tests for COVID – now in custody. Girls were 15 and 16 years of age from NSW.

- **NSW** 21 new cases.

August 12 – **Victoria** deaths 21 – over 400 new cases.

- **Queensland** - no new cases.

August 13 - A **Perth** woman was charged after allegedly avoiding mandatory hotel quarantine when she re-entered Western Australia from Victoria.

Police said the 28-year-old was granted a hard border exemption and was due to arrive at the Perth airport two days ago, however it was alleged she entered the state undetected by road before she was intercepted at her partner's home.

Victoria - 372 new infections and 14 deaths.

- **Victoria** - Homes and social settings are the localities for a significant proportion of Victoria's coronavirus outbreaks during the state's second wave. Abattoirs and warehouses continue to be the workplaces hardest hit by the virus.

Victoria had its deadliest day of the pandemic, with 21 COVID-19 deaths and 410 new cases. There have now been 15,646 confirmed cases of the virus in the state, about half of which are still active infections.

What the Government classes as 'other' outbreaks - student accommodation, backpacker hostels, social outings, with family members account for 5,004 cases from June 1 to August 11. Those infections were found in 369 outbreak hot spots in Victoria.

 - **Western Australia** - Monash University's BehaviourWorks research unit has conducted a national survey of behavioural changes throughout the pandemic. It found that the proportion of West Australians who said they were 'always' practicing social distancing in public has fallen from 61% in April to 38% in early July.

Over the same period, those who said they were 'always' washing their hands for 20 seconds has fallen from 45% to 37%.

August 14 – **Victoria** – 188 people in aged card died this week with 303 new cases and four deaths.

Over 1,000 active cases today. 1,700 military ADF staff working to protect **Melbourne** citizens.

 - Three new cases of people who had been on the **Ruby Princess Cruise Ship** – now a total of 22 deaths and hundreds of cases.

 - **Queensland** - EKKA holiday – **Gold** and **Sunshine Coasts** full of people celebrating EKKA day.

 - **Brisbane** – Story Bridge protest stopped – is now planned for Raymond Park but will likely be cancelled and patrolled by police.

 - A boat with three people crossed the **NSW** border into **Queensland**. They were caught and returned.

 - **NSW** – 9 new cases. Total of 289 deaths – one 20-year-old died.

- **Victoria** - The involvement, or lack thereof, of Australian Defence Force (ADF) personnel in Victoria's Hotel Quarantine program has dominated the politics this week.

The furore was sparked on August 11th when Premier **Daniel Andrews** told a parliamentary inquiry that it was 'fundamentally incorrect to assert that there [were] hundreds of ADF staff on offer and somehow someone said no. That's not, in my judgement, accurate.'

What followed was a swirl of 'duelling statements,' claims and counterclaims. Defence Minister Linda Reynolds came out contradicting Mr. Andrews, saying ADF help was offered multiple times, only to herself be contradicted by Victoria's Emergency Management Commissioner, Andrew Crisp, who said it wasn't offered at a meeting in late March when quarantine was being set up.

– Almost 100 suspect boats in **Queensland** have been stopped by the Maritime Safety Queensland Patrol. Those who were caught were put into self-funded hotel quarantine and each paid $4,003 fines for allegedly making false border declarations. Four people who owned the houseboat were sailing it from Newcastle. 158 people were turned around at the NSW/Queensland border.

- **Western Australia** – Following strict COVID-19 precautions have not only stopped the spread of coronavirus in regional Western Australia, but the precautions have also led to a 95% decrease in the state's influenza cases.

WA Health Department has recorded 216 influenza notifications this year till today, compared to 4,418 at the same time last year, and 429 in 2018.

Flu cases in the metropolitan area have also fallen, with 994 confirmed flu cases so far this year, down from 17,292 in 2019.

Just one person in regional WA and three in the metropolitan area have died from influenza this year.

In 2019 the state recorded 23,210 influenza notifications and 80 deaths - five of which were children under the age of 10.

- There have now been 22,739 cases in **Australia** with 375 deaths - mostly in **Victoria**.

August 15 - **Queenslander** and Epidemiologist, Sophie Rose who is a researcher based in Oxford plans to volunteer to receive a vaccine before being dosed with live coronavirus. Key figures in the study are divided over whether to use the virus. It could be life-threatening – but could bring the vaccine approvals up by six months. The trial could start within weeks if it is approved by their ethics committee.

The study will recruit healthy 20-29-year-olds, whose chances of dying were estimated to be between one in 3,300 to 14,000. The human trial will have four stages:

1. Healthy volunteers receive coronavirus vaccine and begin medical isolation.

2. Two weeks later, or when blood tests confirm they have antibodies, the volunteers are given a controlled live dose of the disease.

3. Volunteers are monitored in laboratory facilities for up to six weeks.

4. The results are provided to health authorities that are considering the vaccine's approval.

– **Brisbane** Hundreds of people turned out for the Refuge Solidarity protest at Kangaroo Point where dozens of asylum seekers were being held in a hotel. Two protesters glued their hands to the road in Walmsley Street, but police removed them using acetone. They were arrested and charged. Another four protesters were arrested, and 12 people were charged. They are planning another protest at Parliament House in Brisbane on August 18th.

August 16 - **Victorian** Premier **Daniel Andrews** spoke to the media at the daily briefing in Melbourne. The state of emergency across Victoria has been extended until Sept. 13.

- **Victoria** reports 282 new cases.

- A sudden surge in the number of coronavirus (COVID-19) cases has been reported from Australian cities of **Melbourne** and **Sydney**.

- **Queensland** - reported another 24 hours with zero new coronavirus cases. There has been 'no evidence' of community transmission in Queensland for 28 days, Premier **Annastacia Palaszczuk** said, and added that it was 'wonderful' news. There was no intention to lift interstate travel restrictions while community transmission was occurring in **Victoria** and **New South Wales,** she said.

Queensland Deputy Police Commissioner Steve Gollschewski said there were 8,800 drivers trying to cross the Queensland border in vehicles over the weekend, of those, 594 people were turned around. There were also 19 airline passengers who were refused entry to Queensland, he said. There were 132 flights which landed in Queensland over the weekend. Of the 7,200 passengers processed, 740 were moved into hotel quarantine. There are currently 3,227 people in Queensland hotel quarantine.

"We're still seeing large numbers of people trying to get into the state that cannot lawfully do so," Deputy Commissioner Gollschewski said.

August 17 - **Sydney** - **NSW** Health declared the City of Sydney a coronavirus hotspot today following recent confirmed cases in the east including at Cafe Peron in Double Bay and the Den Sushi restaurant in Rose Bay. The move comes after the Thai Rock restaurant in Potts Point sparked an outbreak of 37 cases and a number of new infections linked to CBD venues surfaced over the past two weeks.

New South Wales residents are on high alert as case numbers climbed by seven in the 24 hours to 8:00 pm on August 16th, bringing the state's total to 3,768 of which 117 are now active and 54 dead, NSW Health said on Monday night.

August 18 – **Victoria** has recorded 222 new coronavirus cases, the third consecutive day of numbers below 300. The state has recorded 17 further deaths from COVID-19. Today's new case numbers are the lowest in a month, since Victoria recorded 217 new cases on July 18.

- **Queensland** - Premier Annastacia Palaszczuk said yesterday the Government had no intention of opening Queensland's borders to any state or territory that still had community transmission.

With thousands of coronavirus cases still being monitored in Victoria, many of which can be linked to community transmission, as well as an 'accumulation of unsourced cases' in New South Wales, it could take months for those states to reach a point where they can show evidence of zero community transmission.

Ms. Palaszczuk has said she expected a border reopening for Victoria was a shaky prospect this side of Christmas, barring some unforeseen minor miracle.

Economist Nick Behrens from Queensland Economic Advocacy Solutions said, "States like Queensland that have been able to avoid community transmission, are starting to recoup the jobs that were lost."

Mr. Behrens said chasing the tourism dollar from Victoria and New South Wales was still a risky call.

Queensland police figures for last weekend showed there were still people travelling into Queensland from across the country, with 132 flight arrivals.

More than 7,200 passengers were screened, but only 19 were refused entry, while a further 740 people were placed into quarantine.

August 19 - A **Perth** couple posted on Facebook about their attempts to cross interstate borders during the coronavirus pandemic.

Lawrence Gordon Petersen, 63, and Edith van Dommelen, 68, faced the Richlands Magistrates Court in **Brisbane** this morning charged with fraud and failing to comply with border directions.

Police allege the couple falsely declared they had not travelled to a COVID-19 hotspot when they crossed the Goondiwindi border checkpoint on July 27.

That day, Ms. van Dommelen posted to Facebook of their numerous plans to get into Queensland for pet sitting after leaving Victoria. She said they successfully executed 'plan C' which was to exit Victoria with a NSW permit as being in transit, with a separate permit to then enter Queensland.

Ms. van Dommelen said after both permits were approved, they left Victoria with an overnight stay at Wagga Wagga in NSW and decided to do the 'long haul' to enter Queensland on the 27th, ending up in Toowoomba.

On August 5 Assistant Commissioner Steve Gollschewski revealed police had detained the couple in Nanango - where they were pet sitting, after receiving information about the alleged breach.

- **Victoria** – 216 new cases – 12 deaths – all in aged care facilities.

August 20 – **NSW** – 5 new cases.

- **Victoria** – 240 new cases – 13 deaths.

- A **Queensland** youth detention centre is in lockdown after a worker tested positive to COVID-19 as authorities race to find the source of two new mystery coronavirus cases possibly linked to the three women who lied at the border after travelling from Melbourne.

August 21 - Two covidiots who were caught sneaking out of their hotel quarantine to party with a rapper and 'hang out with mates' and gave the media the middle finger as they left **Western Australia.**

Isata Jalloh, 19, and **Banchi Techana**, 22, flew into Perth without permission on August 10th and were told they would need to quarantine before returning to Adelaide. The pair instead left the Novotel Perth a few hours later and caught a taxi to the party at a unit block in Coolbellup, in South Perth.

The women were sent back to **Adelaide** on August 11th and made rude gestures on their way to the airport. Both women had ignored orders from security guards and escaped through Novotel's emergency stairwell around 1.30 am on August 11.

Police had called Jalloh's mobile phone to ask where the women were located but she laughed and hung up on the officer. The mobile phone signal was then used to track both women to the Coolbellup flat occupied by amateur rapper Siri Kidd and a male friend. Both women were arrested around 8.30 am and taken into custody for two days.

They appeared in Perth Magistrate's Court on August 20th and pleaded guilty to the breach. Jalloh was handed a small fine of $5,000 and Techana, who also admitted to obstructing an officer while in custody, was given an eight-month sentence that was sadly suspended for 12 months.

- There are fears coronavirus could quickly spread through a **Brisbane** Youth Detention Centre after several new cases were reported that were linked to a 77-year-old supervisor who unwittingly worked shifts while infectious.

Further testing will be conducted at the facility to determine how the woman contracted the disease. The outbreak is expected to trigger new public health measures in the city.

Queensland Health is yet to rule out any links between the new cases and two young women **Olivia Winnie Muranga** (19), **Diana Lasu** (21) who allegedly lied about returning from Melbourne.

August 23 - A relative of a man who works at the Youth Detention Centre in **Brisbane** tested positive. The man who lives in North Ipswich worked for the centre as well as for a disability accommodation service and tested positive.

 - A female youth detention centre worker from **Forest Lake** tested positive.

Detainees at the centre will be blood tested to find out whether they were the source of the cluster and determine whether any of the detainees came into contact with a trio of Logan women who lied about travelling to Melbourne.

[Author's Note: If this is found to be true, the police should charge the three women with at least endangerment and possibly manslaughter if any of the people who caught the virus died because of their exposure to these very selfish women.]

August 23 – **Victoria** – 208 new cases – 17 death for a total of 502 deaths in the state. A group of 200 people breached the curfew laws. 73 people were given a $1,650 fine.

 - **NSW** – 4 new cases.

 - **Queensland** – 2 new cases. Brisbane declared a 'hot spot' and people warned to look out for illness. 7,000 people were tested for COVID.

August 24 – **Victoria** – 116 new cases – 15 deaths.

August 25 – **Victoria** – 148 new cases - 8 deaths. A flare up in infections in Victoria forced authorities to tighten restrictions on people's movements and order large parts of the state's economy to close but the southeast state has seen a slowdown in new cases in recent days.

Premier Daniel Andrews has defended a plan to extend Victoria's State of Emergency powers that would not see them lifted until September 2021.

The opposition indicated it would not support the bill meaning the premier would need four Upper-House crossbenchers to back it when it was introduced in parliament next week.

The powers would allow the Victoria government to extend a state of emergency in four-week blocks for up to 12 months as well as greater powers to enforce mandatory quarantine, COVID safe plans for businesses and mandatory mask-wearing.

Mr. Andrews defended the plan and argued getting back to normal 'won't ever be an option' if the state could not 'protect what it had already achieved.'

"Extending the State of Emergency is about ensuring that we can legally make the changes our health experts need to keep us safe," he said. "This does not change how long our current lockdown will last or increase the restrictions we face."

August 27 - **Victoria** has confirmed 113 new cases of coronavirus and another 23 deaths. The state's toll is now 485.

- The **South Australian** Premier Steven Marshall stated, "In South Australia, we have opened our borders to Queensland, the Northern Territory, Western Australia and Tasmania. We're looking very closely at the ACT and also New South Wales at the moment. All of our decisions are based on expert health input. We act as soon as we possibly can after receiving that health expert advice."

- **Queensland Health** has expanded its list of venues where cases of the Brisbane Youth Detention Centre cluster visited. Anyone who has been to these locations at the times specified should monitor their health and if they develop any COVID-19 symptoms, even mild ones - get tested.

August 30 – **Wacol**, Queensland – Covid cases tied to the Brisbane Youth Detention Centre and Queensland Corrective Services Academy have now had the following cluster of cases:

August 20 – A woman in her 70s from Bundamba.

August 22 – Men – two in their 40s – one in his 30s. Women – two in their 60s and one in her 20s.

August 23-28 – Men – two in their 30s – one in his 60s. Women – 3 in their 30s, one in her 40s. Male baby under the age of 1.

August 29 – Man in his 30s from Greenbank – Woman in her 30s from Forest Lake – woman in her 30s from Pimpama – woman in her 60s from Forest lake.

 - **Queensland** has recorded four new cases of coronavirus.

Health Minister Steven Miles said all four cases were related to the known COVID-19 outbreak at the Wacol correctional training academy in Brisbane. Mr. Miles said 18,763 Queenslanders had been tested in the previous 24 hours.

"There are 1,060 prisoners on that site and 530 employees," he said.

"Today and tomorrow is a concerted effort in concert with our colleagues at Queensland Health to test those officers on site.

"Of the prison population, we have identified a group that is more at risk than others, 170 or so prisoners, and that's our early work to test those prisoners. All of that work, we hope, will be resolved by this weekend."

August 31 – **Brisbane** and Gold Coast Queensland – restrictions on gatherings and aged care will be extended to the Western Downs, South Burnett, Cherbourg, Toowoomba, Goondiwindi and Southern Downs from 8:00 am today. Queensland Corrective Services Commissioner Peter Martin said that under the Stage 4 lockdown imposed on prisons, prisoners were locked in their cells. About 7,000 prisoners are locked in and they had been compliant with the restrictions so far.

September 1 - **Victoria** has recorded 90 new coronavirus cases yesterday - a slight spike in infections after 58 were reported yesterday. The Health Department also confirmed six more deaths in the past 24 hours.

It comes just hours after a marathon debate ended in the early hours of August 26th, where the Premier's controversial state of emergency extension Bill was passed by a single vote.

The move gives the chief health officer power to ensure the community's safety through detaining people, restricting movement, and preventing entry to premises.

- **Queensland** - Inmates at Arthur Gorrie Correctional Centre in western Brisbane have begun rioting after staff struggled to deliver basic services, including meals and medication, amid a coronavirus lockdown.

Prisoners at the centre have not left their cells for days and have not been able to contact family or their lawyers by phone. Some inmates started lighting fires, smashing windows and flooding their cells with water on Monday in an apparent protest at the deteriorating conditions in the already overcrowded prison.

The prison went into lockdown on August 27th after Queensland Health revealed two of its correctional officers were part of a COVID-19 cluster. Staff were stood down for testing and the first rounds have come back negative.

But a resulting staff shortage left a void that has prompted prison authorities to make a state-wide request for reinforcements from as far away as Lotus Glen Correctional Centre in north Queensland.

– **Queensland** police are investigating an alleged border breach involving notorious former Queensland bikie Shane Bowden who was nabbed at the Brisbane Airport. He said he was not infectious on his flight from Melbourne. Bowden is in hospital amid allegations he lied on his border declaration pass to gain entry into Queensland after reportedly contracting coronavirus.

- A **Queensland** man is in hotel quarantine and is under investigation following an alleged border breach. Police will allege the man travelled from Victoria (Tullamarine Airport) to Brisbane Airport yesterday morning.

As per the current border restrictions, the man returned from a declared COVID-19 hotspot and was placed into hotel quarantine.

Investigations have revealed that the man not only provided false information on his Queensland border declaration but also allegedly breached quarantine in Victoria.

The Queensland Police Service is committed to ensuring everyone complies with public health directions and will continue to enforce restrictions at the border.

Queenslanders have been encouraged to get tested for coronavirus if they experience fever, dry cough or tiredness but one of the state's latest cases has shone a light on the less-common symptoms of the virus.

Yesterday, a 37-year-old man who was employed as a nurse at the Ipswich Hospital tested positive after experiencing abdominal pain.

Health Minister Steven Miles acknowledged that this was one of the rarer symptoms of coronavirus.

"He had identified abdominal pain, which is not normally considered a symptom of COVID-19, but he was incredibly wise, and he identified that could have been a symptom and he went and got tested," Mr. Miles said.

"It underlines how we can all do the right things by monitoring our health and if we have any symptoms at all that are of any cause for concern, we can go and get tested."

- The **AFL Grand Final** won't be hosted in Melbourne for the first time in the game's history. Melbourne Cricket Ground has hosted the AFL Grand Final since 1897, but the game has been relocated due to the city's second COVID-19 wave. Instead, it will be played in Brisbane, with a capped crowd of about 30,000 set to attend on October 24.

September 3 – **Victoria** – 113 new cases – 15 deaths. One-third of these were health care workers. There is a total of 591 deaths in Victoria.

- **NSW** – 12 new cases.

- **Queensland** – 2 new cases, an aged care person in Brisbane and one connected to the Wacol facility.

September 4 – **Canberra** – Scott Morrison urged to prepare new 'hot spot' regulations for locations throughout Australia.

September 5 – **Victoria** – 76 new cases – 11 deaths.

- **Queensland** did not agree with 'hot spot' only bans.

September 6 – **Victoria** 63 new cases – 5 deaths.

- **Queensland** - A woman who was receiving treatment to become a man became pregnant and had to go off her medication while pregnant. While pregnant she caught COVID but was able to have a normal delivery rather than a caesarean birth as was expected because of her COVID.

September 4 - Queensland Police have turned away almost 3,300 motorists at the Gold Coast border since August 8th when travellers from NSW and ACT were barred from entering Queensland except for 'border bubbles' of people straddling the state line. One driver was caught yesterday and fined $4,003 after police discovered a photocopy of someone else's border pass.

- **Ms. Annastacia Palaszczuk** has stated that when NSW and Victoria get things under control – she will open the Queensland borders. There are 25 active cases in Queensland.

Protests September 5

- **Victoria** – Police arrested 17 and will sift through hours of footage of protest chaos to catch more offenders. Hundreds of protesters rioted in the CBD and there was a vicious assault on a police officer. The state recorded 76 new coronavirus infections and 11 deaths.

- **Sydney** – Approximately 1,000 protesters gathered just after five new cases were recorded in NSW with 14 arrested and 81 fines given.

- **Brisbane** – At 2:00 pm 1,500 marched without a single arrest or fine despite only 10 people maximum for gatherings. By late afternoon the numbers dwindled to about 500.

- **Perth** – About 500 people gathered at Parliament house wanting their borders to open up. This city is virtually free of COVID-19.

September 7 - 41 new coronavirus cases in **Victoria** and 9 new deaths.

Melbourne's stage four lockdown has been extended for another two weeks and a significant drop in cases is required before relatively normal businesses operations can resume.

Regional Victoria will move to the second step of the state's roadmap out of lockdown from September 14 due to the low numbers of COVID-19 cases recorded outside of Melbourne. Approximately five per cent of Victoria's coronavirus case count can be found within regional areas, with only 98 active cases found outside the state's capital city. The new changes will allow up to five people from two different households will be allowed to gather outdoors, while all students will begin a staged return to school. Childcare facilities will also reopen and people living alone will be allowed to have a single visitor.

September 9 – **Queensland** – has recorded eight new cases of coronavirus suspected to be linked to existing clusters. Five cases relate to the Wacol cluster, three to the Ipswich hospital. Five of the cases are from the same family, in the same household, and relate to the cluster at the Queensland Correctional Services training academy at Wacol in Brisbane's west. A further three of those cases are linked to a cluster at the Ipswich Hospital, including two healthcare workers already in quarantine and one of their children.

- American actor Tom Hanks has jetted back into the Gold Coast, several months after recovering from coronavirus while down under.

The 64-year-old touched down in a private jet at Coolangatta Airport last night, with photos showing the Hollywood actor walking across the tarmac.

Tom Hanks is back in Australian for the filming of Baz Lurhmann's Elvis Presley film, which is expected to resume at Village Roadshow Studios in Oxenford next month.

September 10 – **Queensland** - A grieving daughter who was banned from attending her father's funeral was surrounded by security guards and dressed in full PPE gear to say her last goodbye.

Canberran Sarah Caisip, 26, was trapped in quarantine in Queensland and was taken under police escort today to see her father's body. She was not able to attend the service.

The heartbreaking 'solution' to a bitter row over the plight of the family was announced by Queensland Health after a war of words between the Prime Minister and the Queensland Premier.

September 13 – **Queensland** – There are three new virus cases including two young girls under 10 years of age and a man in his 20s that are part of the latest cluster which has now included 48 people. The three were close contacts with cases from the Brisbane Youth Detention centre.

- When Queensland can go a fortnight without any confirmed infections outside the protection of quarantine, the outbreak will be considered in check. That will likely be the stimulus for Chief Health Officer Jeannette Young to re-open aged-care and disability accommodation services in SE Queensland.

- Celebrity chef Pete Evans and publisher Pan Macmillan have promoted Evans as being 'the #1 selling Australian health' author. Because of this, the Australian Medical Association has taken aim at him for his stance as an anti-vaccine crusader and for reporting that Covid-19 was a scam. AMA President Dr. Omar Khorshid said, "Pete Evans should stick to writing cookbooks and leave the health advice to people who have actually studied science and medicine at university – not via Google."

- **NSW** Premier Gladys Berejiklian has urged Sydney residents to get tested after the state recorded just nine new cases of COVID-19 overnight.

- **Victoria** – 41 new cases. Premier Daniel Andrews says the state of emergency has been extended for four more weeks, but there will be changes from today. Regional Victoria will take one step today, and they will potentially, around the middle of the week, reach those thresholds of less than five cases, a 14-day average. They are at 4.1 cases now per day," Mr. Andrews said.

"I wanted to remind, as part of that safe and steady steps, part of the roadmap, from 11.59 pm tonight, Melbourne moves from Stage Four restrictions to the first step of our roadmap which brings small, changes that allow for more social interaction and more time outside. Social bubbles for those living alone or single parents - they will be allowed to have one other person in their home.

"Exercise is extended for two hours, split over a maximum of two sessions, but that goes obviously from one hour to two hours, and the notion of time outside, whilst at the moment it is just for exercise, it will also now be from midnight tonight for social interaction with one other person or members of your household.

- The Oxford University virus human testing is now back on. **AstraZeneca** will resume testing 18,000 trial patients. If these are successful, $1.7 billion will purchase 84.8 million doses for Australia. Estimated time frame is early 2021.

September 16 – **Queensland** – Both the Gold Coast and Darling Downs will be allowed to gather in groups of 30 instead of 10 and patients in aged care and hospital facilities will be allowed to have visitors.

Border changes will be discussed on September 18[th.] It is anticipated that if a state goes 14 days with no new cases, their border will likely re-open.

September 17 - Detectives executed a search warrant at a Nerang property last night as a result of investigations into alleged threats made against the Queensland Premier and the Chief Health Officer.

A 43-year-old Nerang man will appear in the Southport Magistrates Court on October 7 charged with one count of Using a carriage service to make a threat to kill.

September 18 - **Victoria** logged 45 fresh cases overnight and five deaths, the highest number of new cases in more than a week, following 28 new cases on September 17th which was the lowest in three months. Unfortunately, the state's number of cases hit a grim new milestone of over 20,000 cases.

 - **South Australian** health authorities are urging residents to better protect themselves once the border to NSW reopens in the next week.

 - The **Western Australia** Premier has agreed to the Prime Minister's request for the state to take on hundreds of international arrivals.

September 19-20 – **Queensland** – no new cases.

September 20 - **Victorian** Police have issued 150 fines in the past 24 hours. 19 of those were for failing to wear a face cover when leaving home for one of the four approved reasons, 10 were at vehicle checkpoints and 42 for breaching curfew.

September 21 – **Victoria** – 11 new cases, 2 deaths

 - NSW – 4 new cases

September 29 - **Victoria** 13 new cases, 4 deaths.

September 30 - Army troops are spending their last day guarding **Queensland's** border, with soldiers to be removed right before the state loosens entry rules for parts of New South Wales. The army will still monitor quarantine hotels.

October 20 – **Victoria -** More than 200 people who underwent hotel quarantine in Victoria must now get tested for HIV and other viruses after a major stuff-up. They have been urged to go get tested for HIV and other viruses after a testing stuff up resulted in possible cross-contamination.

Safer Care Victoria announced yesterday that 243 people who underwent blood glucose level tests while in coronavirus hotel quarantine between March 29 and August 20 could be at risk of contracting a blood borne virus after the same test was used on multiple people.

"Blood glucose level testing devices intended for use by one person were used across multiple residents," Safer Care Victoria said in a statement. "This presents a low clinical risk of cross-contamination and blood borne viruses – Hepatitis B and C, and HIV."

A blood glucose level test involves pricking a finger to get a drop of blood to be used in the testing device.

October 21 - A container ship feared to be carrying a COVID-19 strain never seen in Australia has been prevented from docking in **Brisbane**. The Sofrana Surville is off the Sunshine Coast on Tuesday ahead of testing of the entire crew by Queensland Health the following day.

The New Zealand government alerted Australian officials to the prospect of the ship carrying coronavirus after an engineer who was on another ship, the Ken Rei, tested positive off Napier. The strain of the virus carried by the engineer has not been seen in Australia or New Zealand, the latter nation's authorities say. NZ authorities believe the engineer likely contracted the disease on the Sofrana Surville, where he was on board in Auckland on October 12 and 13.

The ship added fresh crew members from The Philippines on October 13. It then set sail around the Pacific Ocean and was headed for Brisbane. But before it could dock in Brisbane the morning of October 12th, the message reached Queensland Health about the possibility of COVID-exposed crew members.

"No one has left the boat, and no one will leave the boat, until Queensland Health officials give the all-clear around testing results," Federal Agriculture Minister David Littleproud told 7NEWS.

"The New Zealand officials rightfully made contact with the Australian government to alert us. Subsequently, we then notified the Queensland health department to make sure every precaution is taken before we allow anyone to leave that boat. The protocols have worked to the letter."

October 26 - **Victoria** has recorded no new COVID-19 cases and no deaths overnight.

Cases with unknown source are down, and the 14-day rolling average in Melbourne has fallen and remains stable in regional Victoria. But despite the welcome news, Premier Daniel Andrews yesterday said, 'press pause' on the further easing of restrictions.

Yesterday, Mr. Andrews said that the government was awaiting more than 1,000 coronavirus test results from Melbourne's northern suburbs. Last night the Department of Health said they received the results back and all of them were negative.

October 31 - **Queensland** will reopen its border to regional New South Wales on November 3rd but travel from Greater Sydney and Victoria will remain restricted, Premier Annastacia Palaszczuk has announced on the eve of the state election.

November 4 - After months of remaining closed to Victorian residents, **NSW** will drop its border restrictions. Premier Gladys Berejiklian revealed the border would open on November 23. That is about a month after her Victorian counterpart Daniel Andrews put an end to Melbourne's tough stage 4 lockdown.

The southern state has since recorded five consecutive days of zero cases while NSW announced three new local cases today. "As long as a state can demonstrate it can get on top of cases, we are OK with that," Ms. Berejiklian told reporters.

November 9 – No new cases in Victoria, New South Wales and Queensland today. Victoria has had 11 days without a new case.

November 10 - An improved border pass system to streamline the process of entering **Queensland** was introduced today.

With Queensland border restrictions on COVID-19 hotspots of Greater Sydney and Victoria remaining in place, all travellers to Queensland are reminded to apply in advance for a border declaration pass.

The online application process will remove confusion around pass types by auto-selecting passes for applicants based on the information they provide.

All applicants will need to upload supporting documents for validation which may take up to three business days to be processed. Travellers should bring their hard copy documents to border control while the new system is phased in.

There is no need for people with existing Queensland Border Declaration Passes to re-apply as all valid passes will continue to be honoured.

Deputy Commissioner Steve Gollschewski said, "The improvements to the system will further reduce the risk to Queenslanders by strengthening enforcement measures on those who seek to enter our state with false declarations."

November 13 – **Victoria** has reached the extraordinary milestone of no new COVID-19 cases and no further deaths for 14 consecutive days in the wake of its catastrophic second coronavirus wave.

November 17 – **Adelaide** - Authorities are scrambling to contact trace and contain a COVID-19 cluster in Adelaide's northern suburbs, which prompted sweeping new restrictions across the state yesterday.

The new diagnosis brings the number of confirmed and suspected infections associated with the Parafield cluster to 20.

November 29 – **Australia** - New security safety measures that will force all passengers and crew to return a negative COVID-19 test before they can board cruise ships. The sector hopes they will see cruising return by Christmas. Only ships with fewer than 100 passengers will be permitted to enter Australian waters.

December 19 - **Sydney's** Northern Beaches have entered their first day of a crucial five-day lockdown. NSW Premier Gladys Berejiklian announced a stay home order for residents in the affluent region after a cluster linked to the Avalon RSL and Avalon Bowlo grew to 38.

From 5:00 pm today until 11:59 pm on Wednesday, December 23rd, residents must remain home and only leave for essential reasons such as work, shopping, medical care, compassionate grounds and exercise. Anyone breaching public health orders could be slapped with a $1,000 fine.

Ms. Berejiklian also flagged that restrictions could be extended across Greater Sydney if it was warranted.

January 1 - **Victoria** - Acting Premier Jacinta Allan on New Year's Eve announced they will close its border to New South Wales as of 11:59 pm today, prompting a mad dash for Victorian residents to get home. Motorists raced to the border following the announcement, with many ringing in the New Year in lengthy queues. But some unlucky travellers were turned away from border checkpoints minutes after the clock struck 12 today.

Victoria moved swiftly to reinstate mask requirements at all indoor venues a day after its first three coronavirus cases were detected following 60 virus-free days.

January 2 - The **NSW** government backflip on mandating masks in Sydney has been applauded by peak bodies who have called for the change since the first COVID-19 outbreak. Premier Gladys Berejiklian said the reversal in health policy balanced the risk and security to citizens while keeping businesses open.

The Australian Medical Association welcomed Saturday's announcement, which provides for a $200 fine for those breaking the rules.

January 3 – **Queensland** – . Chief Health Officer Dr. Jeannette Young has urged thousands of Queenslanders who returned from Victoria since December 21 to be tested immediately because of the outbreak in Victoria. Those tested must self-isolate at home or in accommodation and can only leave once they have returned a negative result. There is mounting concern around the escalation of cases in NSW and Victoria and the potential for more cases in Queensland. There were 12 new cases in Victoria and NSW had 7 more infections.

January 10 – A Sunday Mail investigation found self-serve checkouts, trolleys, tables and escalators remain covered in high levels of bacteria. A self-serve checkout at a major supermarket recorded the highest level of bacteria.

A mutant South African COVID strain has been detected in four people in NSW prompting stricter hotel quarantine rules. The strain is similar to the UK strain that Queensland authorities are also working to contain finding it is 70% more contagious than the original strain. The AstraZeneca (AZD1222) will be available for use in late February, but the Australian version will take until June. There are over a dozen different tests done on the final product before any batches are released. The Therapeutic Goods Administration has not yet approved the vaccine despite its use in the UK.

This vaccine is a viral vector vaccine, containing a weak or inactivated virus that cannot cause the disease. This virus has genetic material from the COVID-19 virus inserted in it. Once the viral vector is inside human cells, the cells make a protein unique to the COVID-19 virus. This triggers the body to begin to build an immune response.

The pandemic is picking up speed with 14% more cases reported globally per day this week compared to the previous week. Britain approved its third vaccine on January 8th from the US firm Moderna and is rushing to vaccinate as many people as possible.

January 12 – **Queensland** - Police had to escort an angry woman from the John Flynn Private Hospital at Tugun after eagle-eyed staff realised she'd travelled from a Sydney COVID-19 hotspot for a face and breast lift during Queensland's latest border blockade.

January 17 – **Victoria** - Two planeloads of tennis stars and their entourages were sent into hotel lockdown due to three positive cases. 67 passengers were on a Los Angeles flight and 63 on the Abu Dhabi flight and put in hotel quarantine for 14 days. They were not able to train outside their hotel rooms. The Australian Open will start on February 8th.

- Brisbane will clear the way for remaining interstate travel restrictions on Queenslanders to be stopped due to the success of the containment efforts. States and territories slammed their borders shut to the southeast region earlier this month following concerns about the UK strain cluster at the Hotel Grand Chancellor in Brisbane. The NSW border is open to every state and territory, but Western Australia still has a hard border closure to Queensland.

January 23 – **Melbourne** - The world's best tennis players are doing it a bit tough at the moment. They've flown to Melbourne for the Australian Open but have been met with hard quarantine in sometimes less-than-lavish circumstances. Some don't have balconies. One likened it to a prison.

– **Sydney** - More than 180,000 people have been alerted to positive traces of COVID-19 found in sewage in treatments plants located in the west and south-west suburbs of Sydney. A warning was issued today after fragments of the deadly virus were found in the Liverpool and Glenfield treatment plants. The Bureau of Meteorology has forecast severe heatwave conditions for most of NSW with temperatures expected to top 40 degrees Celsius in Sydney's Western Suburbs over the weekend.

"NSW Health urges everyone living or working in these suburbs to monitor for symptoms and get tested and isolate immediately if they appear," health authorities said in a statement.

Positive virus traces were also detected in the Northern Beach sewage plant, as well as in Berala in Sydney's south earlier this week however health authorities said that is likely due to known cases of COVID-19 in the area.

February 12 – **Victoria** - There are fears Victoria's COVID-19 outbreak could spread interstate after an infected person spent more than eight hours at an airport cafe. The Brunetti cafe in Terminal 4 at Melbourne Airport was listed as an exposure site early this morning. It brings the total number of exposure sites listed on the Health Department's website to 30.

The outbreak, connected to the Holiday Inn at Melbourne Airport, has grown to 13 cases, sparking fears the city could again go into lockdown. A total of five new cases were confirmed yesterday, including two announced at 11:00 pm.

February 14 – **Queensland** – 1,500 travellers who entered Queensland on February 9th have been put into isolation after possibly being exposed to a highly infectious strain of COVID-19 at Melbourne's Tullamarine Airport.

February 22 – The first day of vaccines for Australians will be given as follows:

Phase 1a: Quarantine and border workers; frontline healthcare workers; aged-care and disability care staff; aged care and disability care residents.

Phase 1b: Elderly adults aged 80 years and over; elderly adults aged 70-79 years; Other healthcare workers; Aboriginal and Torres Strait Islanders; Younger adults with an underlying medical condition, including those with a disability; clinical and high-risk workers (defence, police, fire, emergency services and meat processing).

Phase 2a: Adults aged 60-69 years; adults aged 50-59 years; Aboriginal and Torres Strait people 18- 54 years; other critical and high-risk workers.

Phase 2b: Balance of the adult population; catch-up period for any unvaccinated Australians from previous phases.

Phase 3: 18 years if recommended.

The first sets will be of Pfizer/BioNTech (20 million doses ordered), then AstraZeneca (53.8 million doses ordered) will be available in early March. Novavax has not been approved in Australia to date, but 51 million doses have been ordered.

CHAPTER 7

FUNNY JOKES

- Quarantine seems like a Netflix series... just when you think it is over, they release the next season.

- I'm starting to like this mask thing... went to the supermarket and two people that I owe money to didn't recognize me.

- Masks are apparently the new bra... They're uncomfortable, you only wear them in public, and when you don't wear one – everyone notices.

- Can someone tell me if the 2nd quarantine will be with the same family... or can we change?

- If you wear a pair of jeans for five days in a row, they become all baggy and it looks as if you are losing weight.

- I still can't believe people's survival instincts told them to grab toilet paper.

- In just two weeks we will hear if there are still two more weeks to let us know that two more weeks of quarantine are needed...

- We want to publicly apologize to the year 2019 for all the bad things we said about it.

- To all the ladies that were praying for their husbands to spend more time with them... how are you doing?

- My washing machine only accepts pyjamas... I put in a pair of jeans and a message came 'stay home!'

- If I see anyone on December 31 crying for this year ending, I will put a bottle to their head!

- After all that we have been through, the only thing missing is that the vaccine will be available only in suppository form.

- I feel like a teenager... no money in my wallet, hair long and out of control, thinking what to do with my life, and grounded at home.

- I had my patience tested. I'm negative.

- You said everything would be back to normal by June. Julyed!

- Lockdown can only go four ways. You'll end up as a monk, a hunk, a chunk or a drunk. Choose how you will end up!

- In life, you will realise there is a role for everyone you meet. Some will test you; some will use you, and some will love you, and some will teach you. But the ones who are truly important are the ones who bring out the best in you. They are the rare and amazing people who remind you why it's worth it.

- 2020 – Weddings: 10 people. Funerals: 10 people. Protests: 1,000 people.

- I'm at that age where my mind still thinks I'm 29, my humour suggests that I'm 12, while my body mostly keeps asking if I'm sure I'm not dead yet.

- It sounds like thunder outside, but the way 2020 is going, it could be Godzilla.

- At the store there was a big X by the register for me to stand on… I've seen too many Road Runner cartoons to fall for that one.

- Keep in mind, even during a pandemic, no matter how much chocolate you eat, your earrings and scarves will still fit.

- I'm going to stay up on New Year's Eve this year; not to see the New Year in, but to make sure this one leaves.

- The dumbest thing I've every purchased was a 2020 planner.

- If I had only known in March that it would be my last time in a restaurant – I would have ordered dessert.

- I never thought the comment, 'I wouldn't touch him/her with a 6-foot pole' would become a national policy, but here we are!

- We've been told that only 5 people are allowed to meet for Christmas, but 15 are allowed for a funeral. We will be holding a funeral for our pet turkey named "Butterball" who will pass away on December 24th, 2020. Refreshments provided. In lieu of flowers and in the spirit of the season please bring a side dish, like a bottle of whiskey, or something similarly healthy!

- It is estimated that the generation born from the global pandemic might be called Covidians, Coronials, or Lockdown Boomers. Australian midwives, gynaecologists and obstetricians are bracing for the busiest influx of births since a decade ago to take place in March, April and May 2021.

- What did our parents do to kill boredom before the internet? I asked my 26 brothers and sisters and they didn't know either.

- Due to my isolation, I finished 3 books yesterday. And believe me – that's a lot of colouring!

- I grew up with Bob Hope, Steve Jobs and Johnny Cash – now there are no jobs, no cash and no hope! Please don't let anything happen to Kevin Bacon!

- I tried donating blood today – never again! Too many stupid questions. Whose blood is it? Where did you get it from? Why is it in a bucket?

- I hate when people forward bogus warnings… This one is real and important! So please send this warning to everyone on your e-mail list. If someone comes to your door saying they are conducting a survey on deer ticks and asks you to take your clothes off and dance around with your arms up – Don't do it! It is a scam – they only want to see you naked. I wish I'd received this yesterday; I feel so stupid now.

- I'm having a quarantine party this weekend. None of you are invited.

- My cousin posted "I'm expecting twins!" I replied, "Finally two kids from the same man."

- My boss arrived at work in a brand-new Lamborghini. I said, "Wow, that's an amazing car!" He replied, "If you work hard, put all your hours in, and strive for excellence, I'll get another one next year."

- When I offer to wash your back in the shower, all you have to say is 'yes' or 'no' – not all this, "Who are you and how did you get in here?"

- Struggling to get your wife's attention? Just sit down and look comfortable.

- I just sold my homing pigeon on EBay for the 22nd time.

I debated about putting this one in, but decided that too many people world-wide would agree with the message:

- Can we just put Donald Trump in a nursing home with a mock-up of the Oval Office and tell him he was re-elected?"

To the citizens of the United States of America from Her Sovereign Majesty Queen Elizabeth II:

"In light of your failure to nominate competent candidates for President of the USA, and thus to govern yourselves, we hereby give notice of the revocation of your independence, effective immediately.

Her Sovereign Majesty Queen Elizabeth II will resume monarchical duties over all states, commonwealths, and territories (except North Dakota, and Utah, which she does not fancy).

Our new Prime Minister, Boris Johnson, will appoint a Governor for America without the need for further elections. Congress and the Senate will be disbanded. A questionnaire may be circulated next year to determine whether any of you noticed.

To aid in the transition to a British Crown dependency, the following rules are introduced with immediate effect:

1. The letter 'U' will be reinstated in words such as 'colour,' 'favour,' 'labour' and 'neighbour.' Likewise, you will learn to spell 'doughnut' without skipping half the letters, and the suffix '-ize' will be replaced by the suffix '-ise.' Generally, you will be expected to raise your vocabulary to acceptable levels. (Look up 'vocabulary').

2. Using the same twenty-seven words interspersed with filler noises such as 'like' and 'you know' is an unacceptable and inefficient form of communication. There is no such thing as US English. We will let Microsoft know on your behalf. The Microsoft spell-checker will be adjusted to take into account the reinstated letter 'u' and the elimination of 'ize.' Microsoft's dictionary will go back to spelling words correctly. For example: correct spelling is: any more – Microsoft anymore; back yard – backyard; back door – backdoor; back seat – backseat; all right – alright; couple of – couple; some place – someplace; and every day – everyday.

3. July 4th will no longer be celebrated as a holiday.

4. You will learn to resolve personal issues without using guns, lawyers, or therapists. The fact that you need so many lawyers and therapists shows that you're not quite ready to be independent. Guns should only be used for shooting grouse. If you can't sort things out without suing someone or speaking to a therapist, then you're not ready to shoot grouse.

5. Therefore, you will no longer be allowed to own or carry anything more dangerous than a vegetable peeler. Although a permit will be required if you wish to carry a vegetable peeler in public.

6. All intersections will be replaced with roundabouts, and you will start driving on the left side with immediate effect. At the same time, you will go metric with immediate effect and without the benefit of conversion tables. Both roundabouts and metrication will help you understand the British sense of humour.

7. The former US will adopt UK prices on petrol (which you have been calling gasoline) of roughly $10/US gallon. Get used to it.

8. You will learn to make real chips. Those things you call French fries are not real chips, and those things you insist on calling potato chips are properly called crisps. Real chips are thick cut, fried in animal fat, and dressed not with catsup but with vinegar.

9. The cold, tasteless stuff you insist on calling beer is not actually beer at all. Henceforth, only proper British Bitter will be referred to as beer, and European brews of known and accepted provenance will be referred to as Lager. South African beer is also acceptable, as they are pound for pound the greatest sporting nation on earth and it can only be due to the beer. They are also part of the British Commonwealth - see what it did for them. American brands will be referred to as Near-Frozen Gnat's Urine, so that all can be sold without risk of further confusion.

10. Hollywood will be required occasionally to cast English actors as good guys. Hollywood will also be required to cast English actors to play English characters. Watching Andie Macdowell attempt English dialect in Four Weddings and a Funeral was an experience akin to having one's ears removed with a cheese grater.

11. You will cease playing American football. There is only one kind of proper football; you call it soccer. Those of you brave enough will, in time, be allowed to play rugby (which has some similarities to American football; but does not involve stopping for a rest every twenty seconds or wearing full Kevlar body armour like a bunch of nancies).

12. Further, you will stop playing baseball. It is not reasonable to host an event called the World Series for a game which is not played outside of America. Since only 2.1% of you are aware there is a world beyond your borders, your error is understandable. You will learn cricket, and we will let you face the South Africans first to take the sting out of their deliveries.

13. You must tell us who killed JFK. It's been driving us mad for many years.

14. An internal revenue agent (i.e. tax collector) from Her Majesty's Government will be with you shortly to ensure the acquisition of all monies due (backdated to 1776).

15. Daily Tea Time begins promptly at 4:00 pm with proper cups, with saucers, and never mugs, with high quality biscuits (cookies) and cakes; plus strawberries (with cream) when in season.

God Save the Queen!

I tried this Covid 19 Test and it truly works !!

A new and easy test for the horror of Covid 19 is doing the rounds and it's simple, quick and positive (or negative if you see what I mean).

Take a glass and pour a decent nip of your favourite Single Malt Scotch into it; then see if you can smell it.

If you can, then you are halfway there.

Then drink it.

If you can taste it then it is reasonable to assume you are currently free of the virus because the loss of the sense of smell and taste is a common symptom.

I tested myself 7 times last night and was virus free every time thank goodness.

I will have to test myself again today because I have developed a throbbing headache which can also be one of the symptoms.

I'll report my results later.

Smell

I went out for a New Years' walk with my new girlfriend and we saw dogs mating.

She said: "How does the male know when the female is ready for sex?"

I replied: "He can smell she is ready That's how nature works."

We then walked past a sheep field and the ram was mating the ewe.

Again, my girlfriend asked: "How does the ram know when the ewe is ready for sex?"

I replied: "It's nature. He can smell she is ready."

We then went past a cow-field and the bull was mating with the cow.

My girlfriend said: "This is odd. They are really going at it. Surely the bull can't smell when she is ready?"

I said: "Oh, yes; it's nature. All animals can smell when the female is ready for sex."

Anyway, after the walk, we stopped at her door and I kissed her goodnight.

She turned back from the door and said: "Take care and get yourself checked out for Covid-19."

Surprised, "Why do you say that?" I asked her.

She replied: "You seem to have lost your sense of smell."

Quarantine in Victoria, Australia

I've finally worked out the story of the hotel quarantine bungle in Victoria.

There were four people responsible named Everybody, Somebody, Anybody and Nobody.

There was an important job to be done and Everybody was sure that Somebody would do it.

Anybody could have done it, but Nobody did it.

Somebody got angry about that, because it was Everybody's job.

Everybody thought Anybody could do it, but Nobody realised that Everybody wouldn't do it.

It ended up that Everybody blamed Somebody when Nobody did what Anybody could have.

I'm glad I cleared that up for you all.

The positives of lockdown:

Traffic has gone,

Fuel is affordable,

Bills are extended,

Kids are home with their families,

Parents are at home looking after their families,

Fast food is replaced with home cooked meals,

Don't have to go to work every day,

Hectic schedules replaced with naps, rest, and relaxation,

The air seems cleaner,

The world is quieter,

People are conscious about hygiene and health,

Money doesn't make the world go round any more,

Designer clothing is pointless because nobody sees what you wear,

Doctors and nurses are being praised and recognised instead of celebrities,

We finally have time to smell the roses,

We take time to look up at the stars,

Our world is pretty amazing.

CHAPTER 8
FUN PICTURES

SOCIAL DISTANCE SERVICE DOGS

AVAILABLE WHILE SUPPLIES LAST

So in retrospect, in 2015, not a single person got the answer right to "Where do you see yourself 5 years from now?"

Our owner was just tested for COVID-19

I'm not adding this year to my age
- I didn't use it!

All these humans with muzzles! Who did they bite?

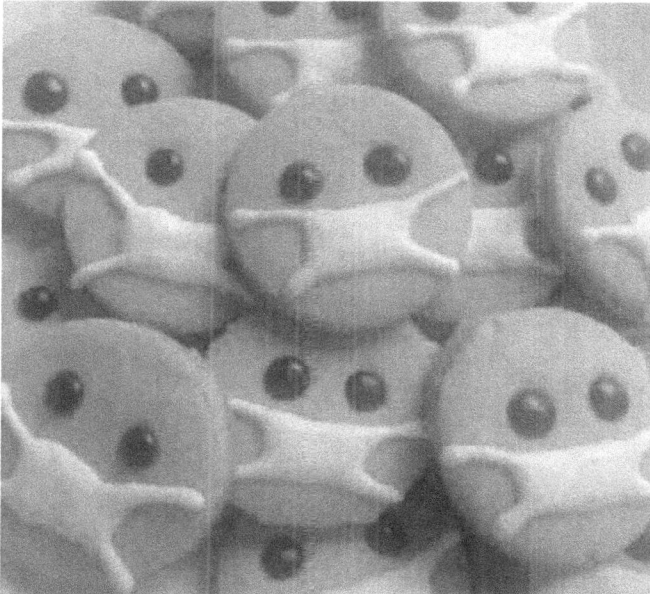

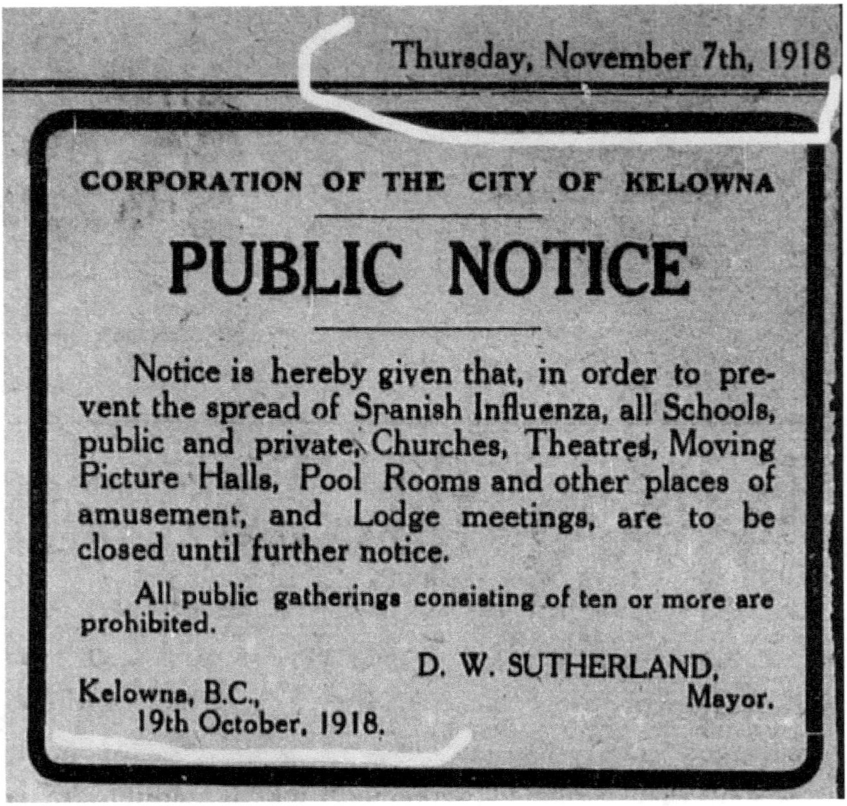

Thursday, November 7th, 1918

CORPORATION OF THE CITY OF KELOWNA

PUBLIC NOTICE

Notice is hereby given that, in order to prevent the spread of Spanish Influenza, all Schools, public and private, Churches, Theatres, Moving Picture Halls, Pool Rooms and other places of amusement, and Lodge meetings, are to be closed until further notice.

All public gatherings consisting of ten or more are prohibited.

D. W. SUTHERLAND,

Kelowna, B.C.,   Mayor.
   19th October, 1918.

Like a Good
Neighbor
Stay Over There

WARNING

BARS NEED YOUR HELP
WE CAN ONLY OPEN AT
1/3 OF OUR CAPACITY!

THOSE WHO CANNOT
DRINK FOR 3
ARE KINDLY ASKED TO
LEAVE THEIR PLACE TO THE
PROFESSIONALS!!

Good morning. What are we offended by today?

Toilet paper is the new currency.

It's called butt-coin!

Coronavirus throat spray

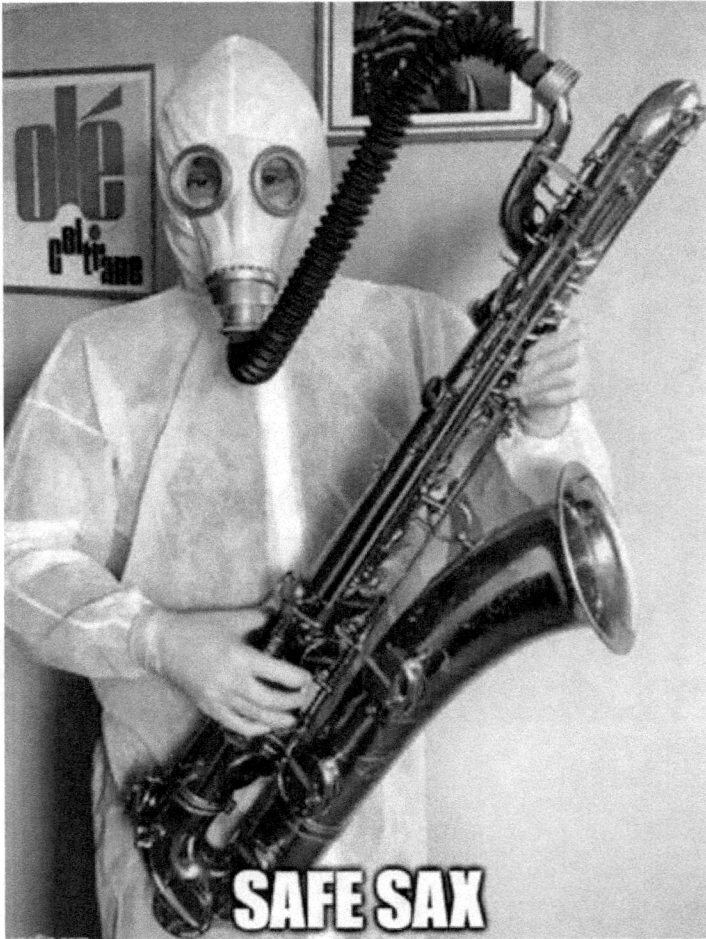

SAFE SAX

Not in my wildest dreams did I imagine myself entering a bank, wearing a mask and asking for money.

After a two-year loan to the United States, Michelangelo's David is being returned to Italy.

But somehow, he looks different after COVID-19.

Romance novels written
during Covid-19
will be like...
"And then she slowly
slipped her mask down,
revealing her warm red
lips, and her blushed face,
and as their eyes met, he
gently removed her gloves."

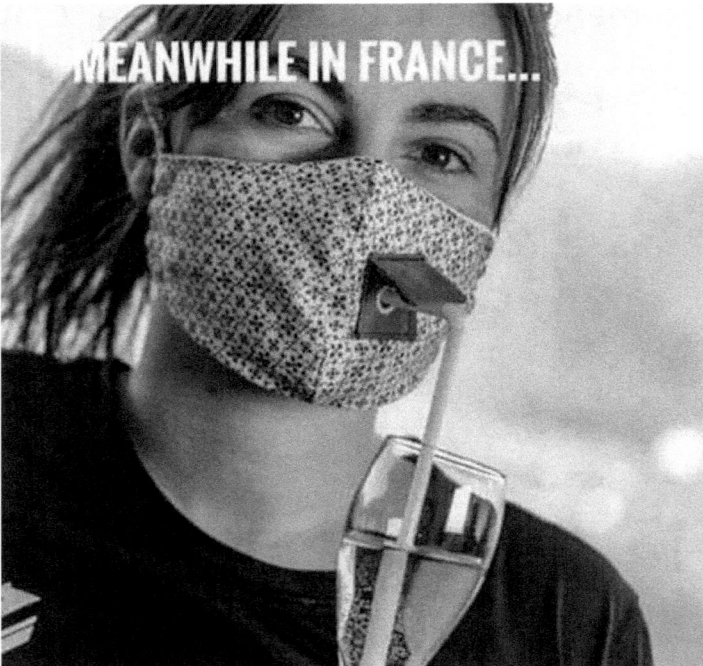

MEANWHILE IN FRANCE...

If you used one of these:

Stay at home! You are in the high risk group.

I recently bought a toilet brush......

long story short, I'm going back to toilet paper

PRETTY WILD HOW WE USED TO EAT CAKE AFTER SOMEONE HAD BLOWN ON IT... GOOD TIMES....

Ran out of toilet paper and now using lettuce leaves.
Today was just the tip of the iceberg, tomorrow romaines to be seen.

The police said he was nuts!

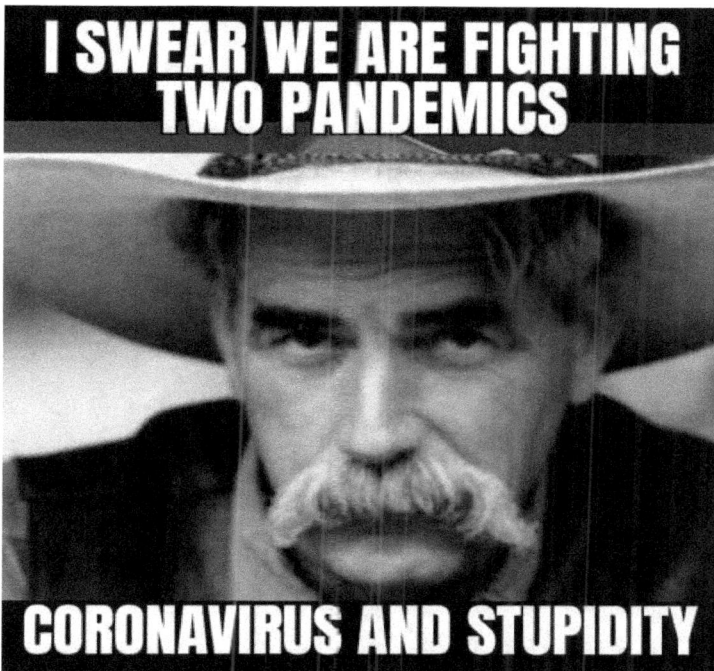

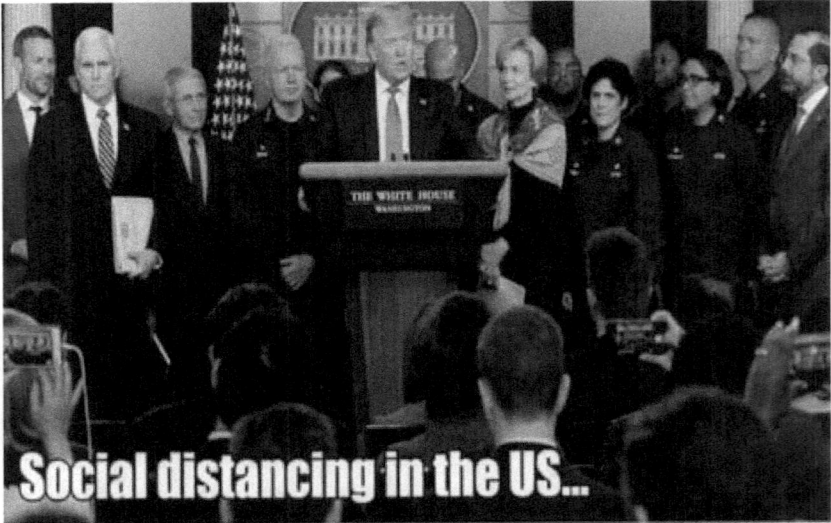

Now that we know who the essential workers are, explain to me why Professional Athletes make so much more money if they are basically useless when it matters.?

New corporate problems

"OK, which one of you just called me an asshole?"

Department of health
is looking to hire
couples married for
7 years or more to
educate people on
social distancing.

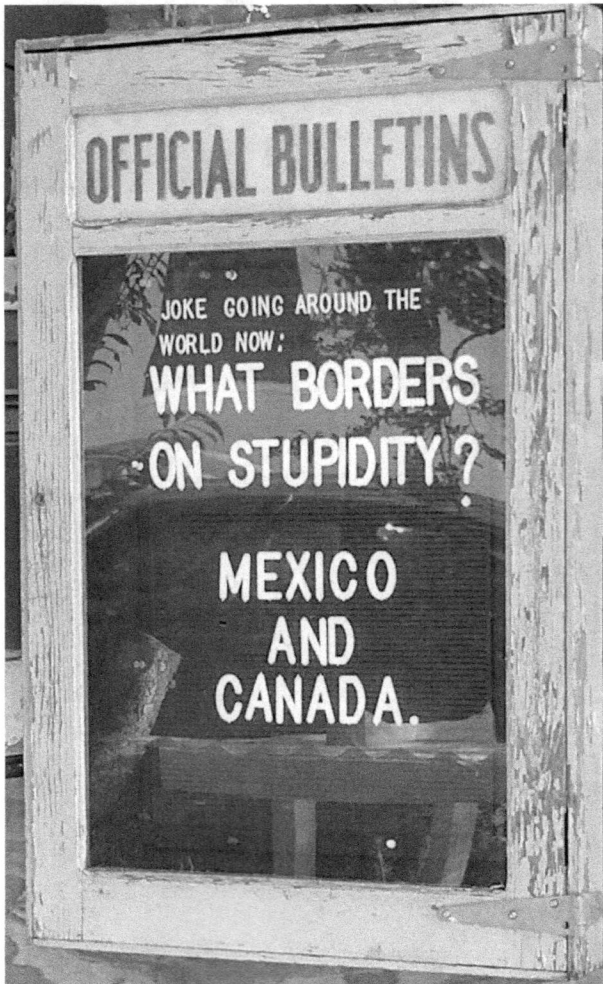

OFFICIAL BULLETINS

JOKE GOING AROUND THE
WORLD NOW:
WHAT BORDERS
ON STUPIDITY?

MEXICO
AND
CANADA.

A British doctor says: "In Britain, medicine is so advanced that we cut off a man's liver, put it in another man, and in 6 weeks, he is looking for a job."

The German doctor says: "That's nothing, in Germany we took part of a brain, put it in another man, and in 4 weeks he is looking for a job."

The Russian doctor says: "Gentlemen, we took half a heart from a man, put it in another's chest, and in 2 weeks he is looking for a job."

The American doctor laughs: "You are all behind us. A few months ago, we took a man with no brain, no heart, and no liver and made him President.

Now, the whole country is looking for a job!"

Who was complaining that 2020 didn't have enough holidays... Now what?

Spotted in London, UK…

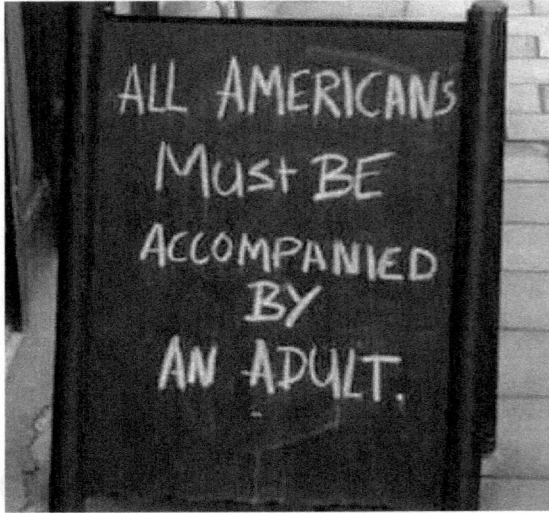

All AMERICANS
Must BE
ACCOMPANIED
BY
AN ADULT.

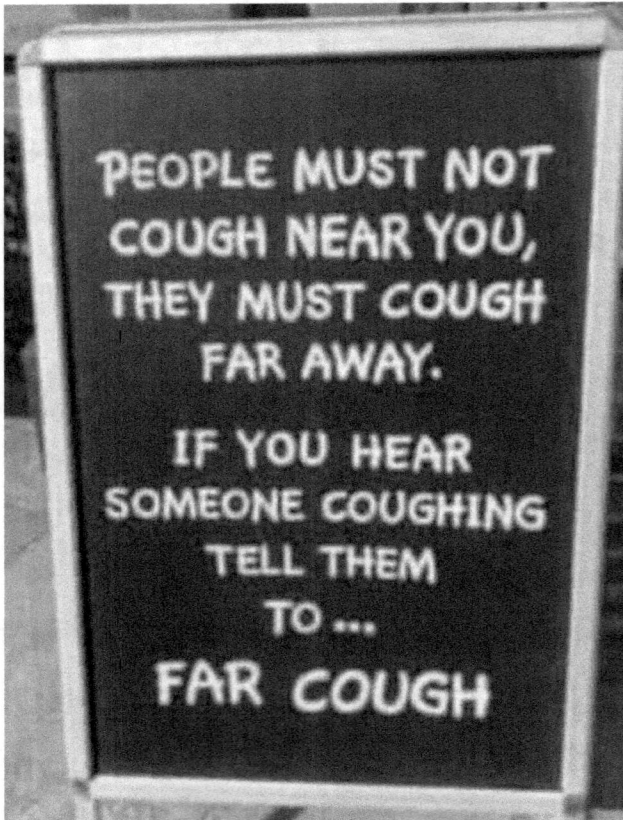

PEOPLE MUST NOT
COUGH NEAR YOU,
THEY MUST COUGH
FAR AWAY.

IF YOU HEAR
SOMEONE COUGHING
TELL THEM
TO …
FAR COUGH

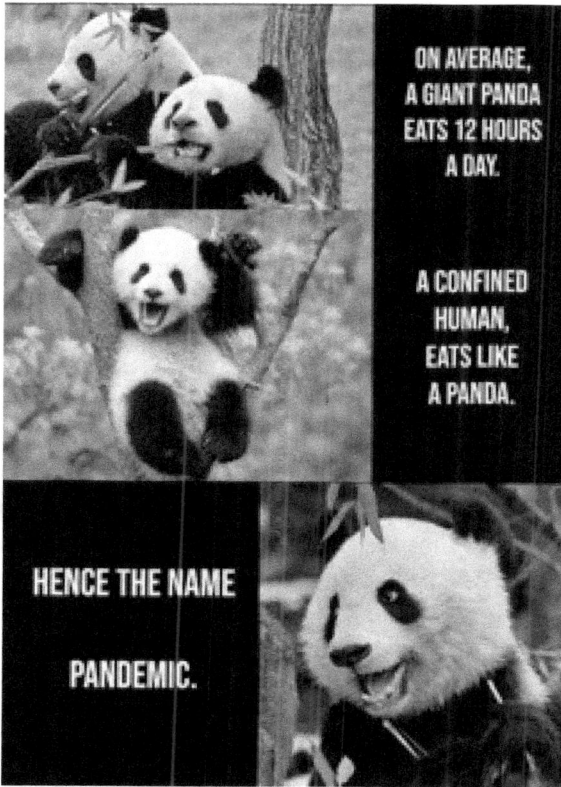

ON AVERAGE,
A GIANT PANDA
EATS 12 HOURS
A DAY.

A CONFINED
HUMAN,
EATS LIKE
A PANDA.

HENCE THE NAME

PANDEMIC.

Tan lines in 2020

You never appreciate what you have till it's gone.
Toilet paper is a good example.

Husband and I went grocery shopping with masks, got home, took off masks, brought home wrong husband! Stay alert people!

**Dear Lord,
Please don't let Brussel Sprouts
be a part of the cure of Covid-19 Virus.**

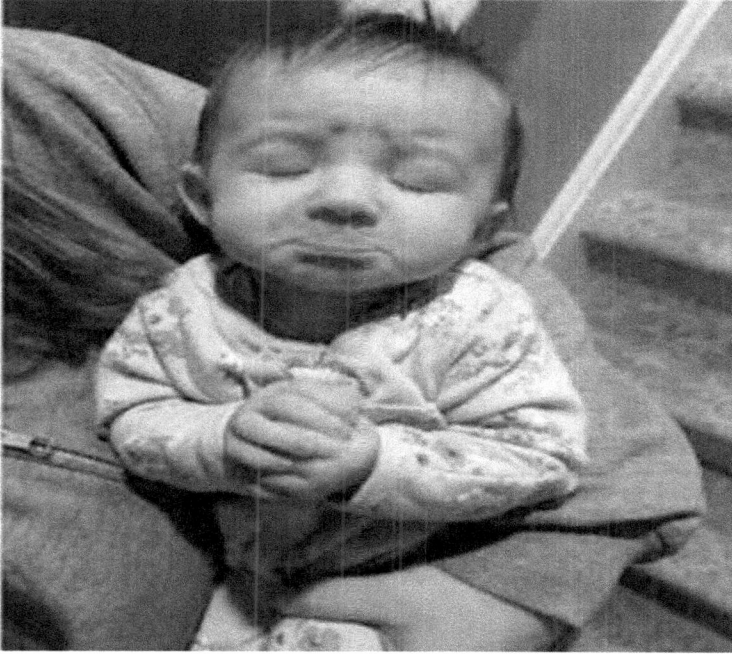

Nine months past Corona:

Who is the father?

Don't know; he wore a mask!

Please don't leave me at grandma's place again!

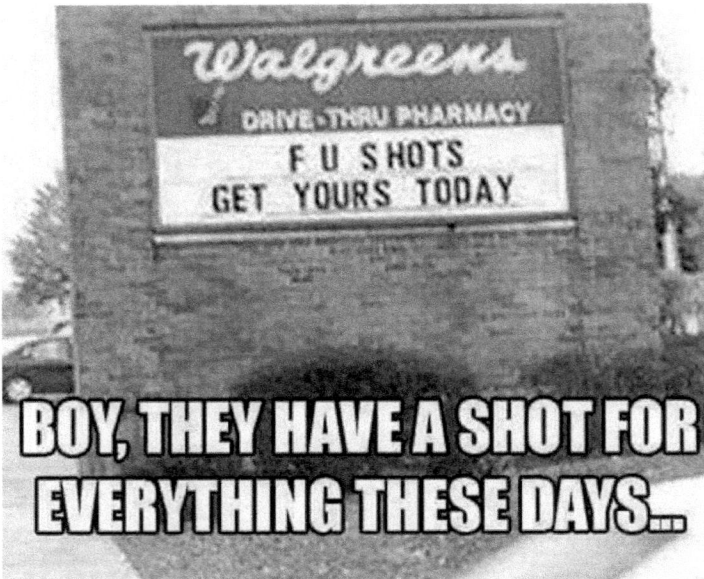

Don't let them take the temperature on your forehead as you enter the supermarket, its a government plot to erase your memory. I went for a bottle of milk and a loaf of bread and came home with a case of beer and 12 bottles of wine!

DAMN TACOS

Add a New Payment Method

○ **Add New Card** VISA mastercard DISCOVER AMEX

○ VISA Pay with VISA

○ PayPal Pay with PayPal

◉ Pay with Toilet Paper

Continue with ToiletBank

On the floor in a Tim Horton's in
Newmarket, Ontario, Canada.

All right – does everyone have sound?

CLEANED THE TV SCREEN WITH ANTI-VIRUS WIPES

LOST BBC NEWS, SKY NEWS & CHANNEL 4 NEWS.

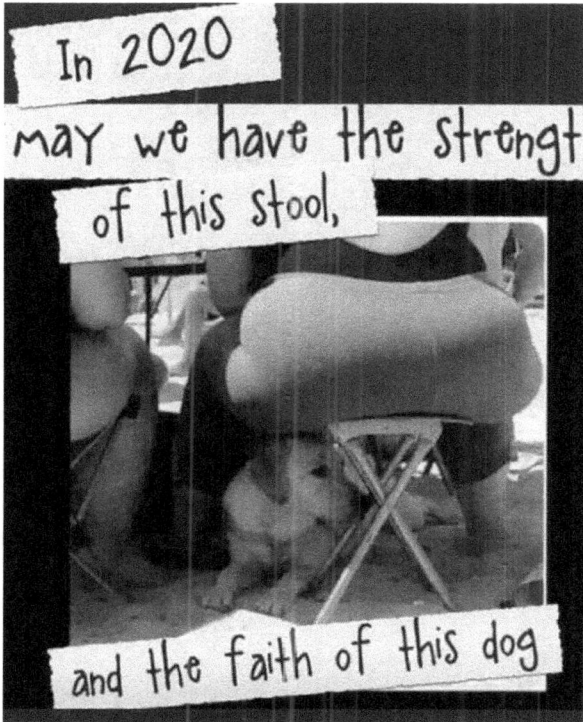

In 2020 may we have the strength of this stool, and the faith of this dog

The King of Spain has been quarantined on his private jet.

That means the reign in Spain stays mainly on the plane...

COMING DECEMBER 2020

KORONA AND KWARENTINE

HOW MUCH SHOULD YOU SPEND ON A BOTTLE OF WINE?

I DON'T KNOW...

HALF AN HOUR?

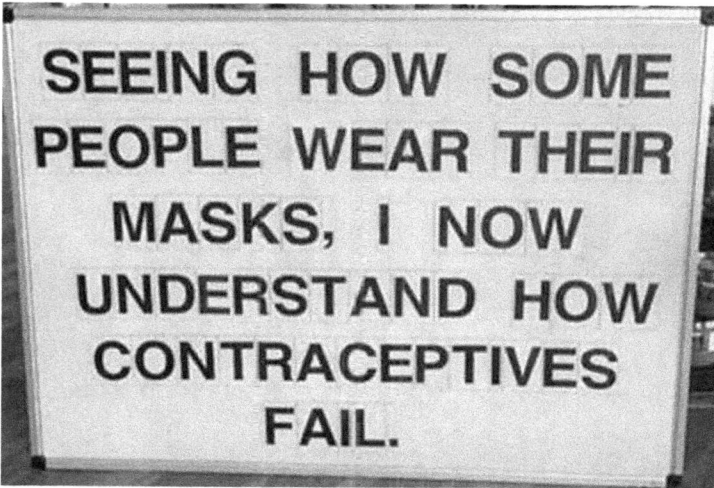

SEEING HOW SOME PEOPLE WEAR THEIR MASKS, I NOW UNDERSTAND HOW CONTRACEPTIVES FAIL.

When history books try to explain why a country with 4% of the world's population managed to account for over 25% of the world's COVID19 deaths, I suggest they use this picture:

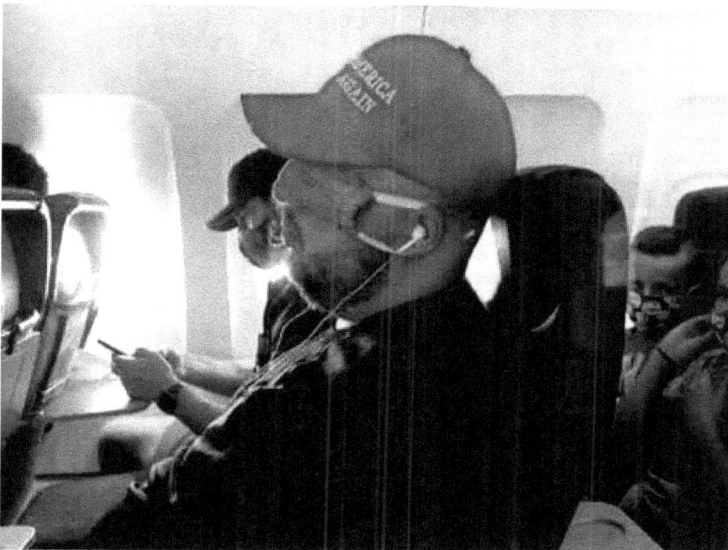

They say you can't fix
STUPID
★TURNS OUT★
You Can't
QUARANTINE
★★ IT EITHER ★★

In other news...
the Seven Dwarfs
have been advised
that as of today,
they can only meet in
groups of six.
One of them isn't
Happy.

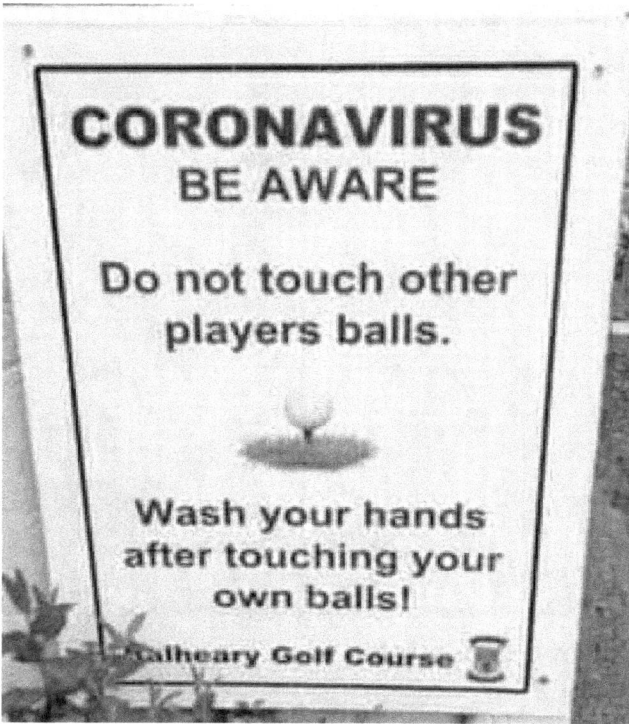

CORONAVIRUS
BE AWARE

Do not touch other
players balls.

Wash your hands
after touching your
own balls!

Calheary Golf Course

When the doctor says you need to watch your drinking

GLOBAL WARMING

It's not a Covid joke, but I just couldn't resist.

Stock up on Home Schooling Supplies Here

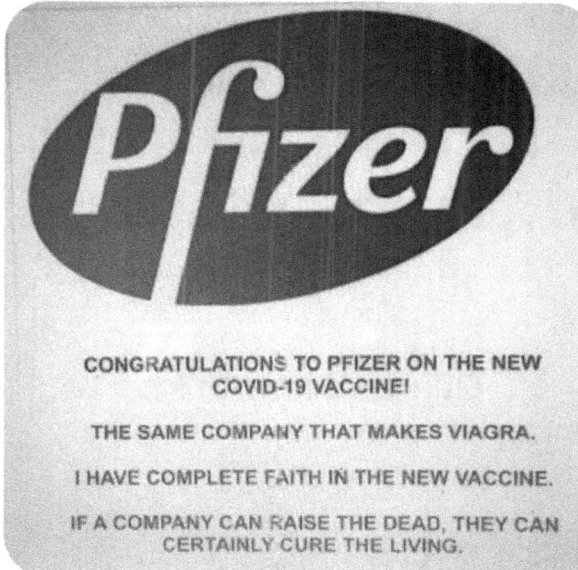

CONGRATULATIONS TO PFIZER ON THE NEW
COVID-19 VACCINE!

THE SAME COMPANY THAT MAKES VIAGRA.

I HAVE COMPLETE FAITH IN THE NEW VACCINE.

IF A COMPANY CAN RAISE THE DEAD, THEY CAN
CERTAINLY CURE THE LIVING.

Now there's an idea.

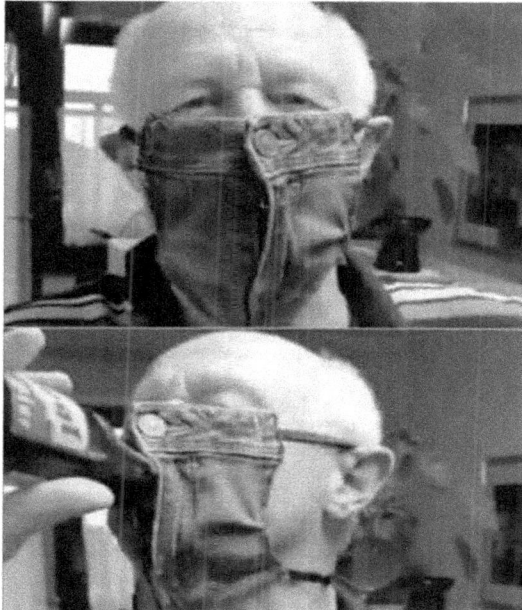

If you're refusing to wear a
mask due to concerns your
brain won't get enough
oxygen, I think that ship has
already sailed. 😊

Quarantine with kids...

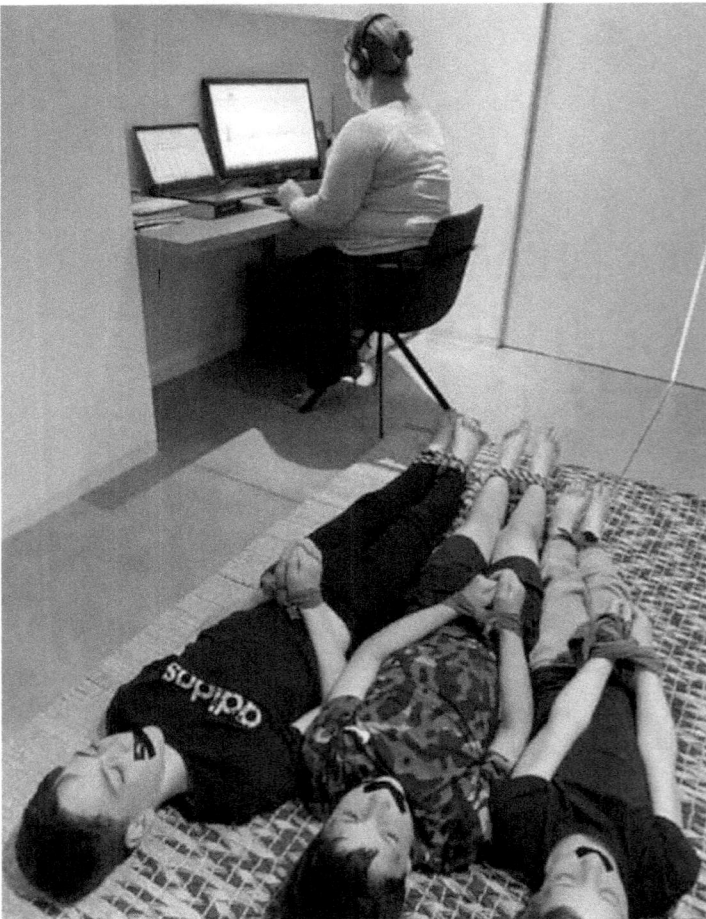

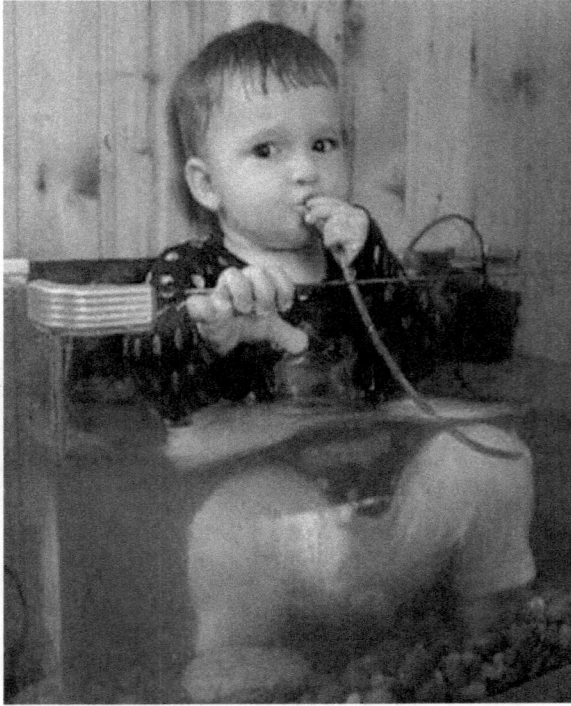

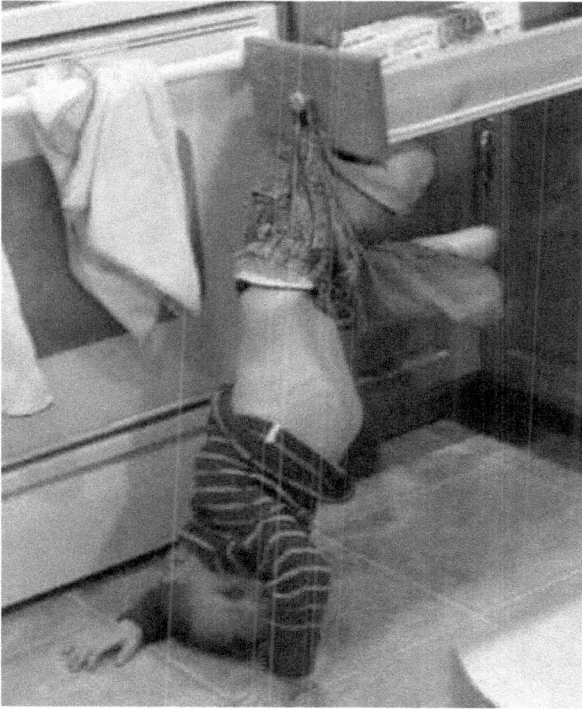

CHAPTER 9

WHAT'S IN THE FUTURE

It's been a long, hard, bumpy road the past 400 days. Everyone world-wide has been affected by the pandemic and it's not over yet. One wonders how long the virus will still be around and whether the different vaccines will work on the new strains.

And what will happen in the US now that a more mature president is at the helm. One also wonders whether Donald Trump will be kept out of politics by failing to have a duty of care towards the health of the US population by refusing to use or encourage citizens to follow pandemic safety measures. He needs to take serious responsibility for the 517,204 deaths that have occurred so far. If he had given proper leadership and insisted on safety measures, I'm sure the number of cases would have been halved. He should have this gnawing on his conscience (if he has one).